TWAYNE'S WORLD AUTHORS SERIES
A Survey of the World's Literature

HUNGARY

Enikő Molnár Basa, American University

EDITOR

Imre Madách

TWAS 617

Imre Madách

IMRE MADÁCH

By DIETER P. LOTZE
Allegheny College

TWAYNE PUBLISHERS
A DIVISION OF G. K. HALL & CO., BOSTON

Copyright © 1981 by G. K. Hall & Co.

Published in 1981 by Twayne Publishers,
A Division of G. K. Hall & Co.
All Rights Reserved

Printed on permanent/durable acid-free paper and bound
in the United States of America

First Printing

Library of Congress Cataloging in Publication Data

Lotze, Dieter P.
Imre Madách.

(Twayne's world authors series; TWAS 617)
Bibliography: p. 163–67
Includes index.
1. Madách, Imre, 1823–1864—Criticism and interpretation.
2. Madách, Imre, 1823–1864. Az ember tragédiája.
3. Romanticism—Europe.
I. Title. II. Series.
PH3281.M15Z735   894'.51122   81-2055
ISBN 0-8057-6459-3   AACR2

Feleségemnek: For my wife

Contents

About the Author

Dieter P. Lotze was born in Hanover, Germany, in 1933. After the Gymnasium in Celle, he studied German and English philology and literatures as well as comparative literature at West Berlin's Free University and at Innsbruck University where he obtained his doctorate with a dissertation on Imre Madách which earned him the Südosteuropa-Institut, Munich, award for the best scholarly work on Southeastern Europe. He began his teaching career in the United States in 1961 as Instructor in Modern Languages at Allegheny College where he is presently holding a position as Professor of Modern Languages. He also taught as Visiting Professor of German at Colorado College. His special research interests are nineteenth-century literature in Germany and in Hungary, comparative literature studies, and the methodology of language instruction. He is the author of *Wilhelm Busch* in the German section of Twayne's World Authors Series, and his articles on pedagogy and on literature (Busch, Celan, Goethe, Heine, Victor Hugo, Kafka, Lessing, Thomas Mann, Madách, and Hungarian Romanticism) have appeared in publications in the United States, Canada, Germany, Hungary, and Japan.

Preface

Imre Madách's dramatic poem *Az ember tragédiája (The Tragedy of Man)* holds a special place in Hungarian culture. Magyars generally see it as the most outstanding combination of philosophy and literature ever produced in their language. Its deliberate universality—already indicated in its title—sets it apart from most Hungarian literary works and makes it more easily accessible to foreigners. On the surface, only its language seems to separate it from the writings of other European poets. Yet for many generations Hungarians have considered it very much as part of their cultural heritage and expressive of their national experience.

As the first book in English on Imre Madách and his work, this monograph will attempt to provide a general introduction. It is my hope that the reader will gain some insight into the complexity of the poet and his creation. I also intend this book as a memorial to the three eminent literary historians who offered guidance to my first Madách studies more than twenty years ago: Karl Kurt Klein, Béla Zolnai, and Marcell Benedek. While I am sure none of them would agree with everything I am setting forth here, I am equally convinced that they would be gratified by my continued effort to win a wider audience for a writer who is still too little known beyond the borders of his native land.

There is no such thing as total objectivity in dealing with literature. My own biases will quickly become clear to the reader, but I might as well admit to some preconceived notions at the outset. This study will reflect three basic assumptions: Madách is the author of a single outstanding literary work. Madách, the man and the writer, was deeply affected and shaped by experiences in his personal life and in the life of the nation, but—as in the case of all truly great artists—his poetic work transcends the realm of the individual. Madách was a Hungarian patriot and an exponent of national culture as well as a citizen of the world and an heir to the traditions of Western Europe.

Translated into the specifics of the present monograph, these assumptions mean: Madách's *Az ember tragédiája* will be discussed almost to the total exclusion of his other literary production. A very superficial overview will be given of his poetry, his prose narratives, and his other dramatic attempts, but throughout the book they will be viewed chiefly in their relation to his one masterpiece. My critical judgment in this respect seems to be shared by the overwhelming majority of scholars, and even the recent public acceptance of Madách's Moses drama does not change the fact that he is essentially a one-work writer.

The playwright's life will be outlined, and there will be numerous references to events that had an impact on him, but his work will not be treated as the simple and immediate result of his experiences or as fictionalized autobiography. Since Madách—like so many Hungarian writers—was actively involved in the public and political life of his country, and since his poetic production should be seen against the backdrop of his times, a thumbnail sketch of Hungary in the nineteenth century and of historic developments of major importance is given as an aid to the non-Magyar reader. But again, *Az ember tragédiája* will not be interpreted as a disguised representation of contemporary conditions.

Perhaps most important, it is my conviction that Hungarian literature in general, that of the nineteenth century in particular, and most of all the work of Imre Madách should be seen in a European context. By outlining a wider framework, by tracing parallel trends in other countries, and by analyzing mutual impacts across national and linguistic borders, his accomplishment is not diminished but rather enhanced. At the same time Madách's position in the peculiar development of Hungarian literature will not be overlooked.

Parenthetical page references in the text are to the translation by Charles Henry Meltzer and Paul Vajda, *The Tragedy of Man* (Budapest: Corvina Press, 4th ed., 1960). Those preceded by the abbreviation "ÖM" are to volume and page numbers of the collected edition, *Összes művei*, ed. Gábor Halász (Budapest: Révai, 1942). Unless otherwise indicated, all translations are my own.

DIETER P. LOTZE

Allegheny College

Acknowledgments

I gratefully acknowledge the permission of Corvina Kiadó to quote from Imre Madách, *The Tragedy of Man: A Dramatic Poem in Fifteen Scenes*, translated by Charles Henry Meltzer and Paul Vajda (4th edition, Budapest, 1960), and that of W. W. Norton & Company to cite from Johann Wolfgang von Goethe's *Faust: A Tragedy*, translated by Walter Arndt, edited by Cyrus Hamlin (A Norton Critical Edition, Copyright © 1976 by W. W. Norton & Company, Inc., New York). György M. Vajda, editor of *Neohelicon* (Budapest), graciously granted me the right to use my two articles from that journal (see Bibliography) in the sixth chapter of this book. I am obliged to Allegheny College for supporting my work through a sabbatical leave and for some financial aid. In addition, I owe thanks to many individuals. Enikő Molnár Basa, editor of the Hungarian Section of Twayne's World Authors Series, made this monograph possible through her confidence, patience, and helpful comments. Vera Crispin rendered invaluable aid in the preparation of the manuscript. István Sőtér, János Barta, Károly Horváth, and Andrew Török offered encouragement and suggestions or made useful resources available to me. Judit Karafiáth, Foreign Relations Secretary of the Institute for Literary Studies, Hungarian Academy of Sciences, provided me with important material and was always willing to assist. But most of all I would like to thank my wife and collaborator Barbara. Without her advice, help in translation, encouragement, and overall support, this book could not have been written.

Chronology

1823   Imre Madách born on January 21 at Alsósztregova, Nógrád County (today Dolná Strehová, Czechoslovakia).

1834   Death of his father.

1837   Completion of secondary school in Pest and matriculation at the university to study philosophy, later also law.

1839   Publication of his first poem, "Az anya gyermeke sírján" (The Mother at Her Child's Grave), in *Honművész*.

1840   Publication of *Lantvirágok* (Lyre Blossoms), twenty-six poems written for Etelka Lónyay. Madách leaves Pest for health reasons and later continues his studies at Alsósztregova.

1841–
1842   Dramas: *Commodus; Nápolyi Endre* (Andrew of Naples).

1842   After successful bar examination, Madách accepts appointment as Deputy Clerk for Nógrád County at Balassagyarmat. Essay fragment: "Művészeti értekezés" (Discourse on Art). Story: "Duló Zebedeus kalandjai" (Zebedee Duló's Adventures).

1843   Honorary County Notary. Resignation after a short period due to health problems. Dramas: *Férfi és nő* (Man and Woman); *Csak tréfa* (Just a Joke).

1843–
1845   Drama fragment: *Jó név és erény* (Good Reputation and Virtue). Stories: "Az ecce homo" (The Ecce Homo); "Krónika két pénzdarab sorsáról" (Chronicle of the Fate of Two Coins); "Hétköznapi történet" (Everyday Story).

1844   County Court Judge. Centralist leader in the County Assembly. Coauthor of satirical epigrams, "Nógrádi képcsarnok" (Nógrád Picture Gallery), with Pál Szontágh and Ferenc Pulszky.

1844–
1847   Several reports and articles for *Pesti Hírlap*.

1845   Marriage with Erzsébet (Erzsi) Fráter. Madách moves to the family estate at Csesztve.

1846   Election as Chief Commissioner of Nógrád County; resignation in 1847 because of poor health.

1848– Health reasons prevent Madách from active participation in
1849   the war. His sister Mari and her family are brutally murdered
       by Rumanian terrorists. His brother Pál dies on his way to join
       Kossuth after Nógrád has surrendered.
1851   Madách gives shelter to a political fugitive.
1852   Arrest and imprisonment for almost a year at Pozsony
       (Bratislava) and Pest.
1853   Release from prison in May. After a period of being restricted
       to Pest, Madách returns to Csesztve in the fall, later moves to
       Alsósztregova.
1854   Divorce from Erzsi.
1855   Revision of 1843 drama, *Mária királynő* (Queen Mary).
1859   Drama: *A civilizátor* (The Civilizer).
1859– Drama: *Az ember tragédiája (The Tragedy of Man).*
1860
1860   Election as representative of Balassagyarmat at the 1861 Diet
       in Pest. Drama: *Mózes* (Moses).
1861   Revision of 1843 drama, *Csák végnapjai* (Csák's Last Days).
       Important parliamentary speeches.
1862   Election to the Kisfaludy Society. Inaugural address: "Az aes-
       thetika és társadalom viszonyos befolyása" (The Mutual Im-
       pact of Esthetics and Society). Publication of *Az ember
       tragédiája* by the Kisfaludy Society.
1863   Election as corresponding member to the Academy of Sci-
       ences.
1864   Inaugural address before the Academy (read by a friend be-
       cause of Madách's failing health): "A nőről, különösen aes-
       thetikai szempontból" (On Woman, Particularly from an Es-
       thetic Viewpoint). Story "A Kolozsiak" (The Kolozsi Family)
       published in *Koszorú*. Drama fragment: *Tündérálom* (Fairy
       Dream). On October 5, Madách dies at Alsósztregova of heart
       failure.
1883   First performance of *Az ember tragédiája* (arranged for the
       stage by Ede Paulay) at the National Theater in Budapest.

CHAPTER 1

Imre Madách's Life and Times

I Hungary in the Nineteenth Century

ANY literary study can be enriched by a glance at the prevailing economic and political conditions and at historical developments. In the case of Hungarian literature—particularly of the nineteenth century—at least a cursory investigation of this background appears indispensable. Hungary's experiences between the death of Maria Theresia and the Compromise of 1867 were traumatic, and far-reaching changes occurred during this period. And Hungarian men of letters were among their country's most outstanding political activists. A brief look at some writers of the first half of the century will illustrate this almost unequaled degree of political engagement.

Two of the men imprisoned in 1795 after the abortive plot of Abbé Martinovics were Ferenc Kazinczy, whose language reform was to lay the foundation for modern Hungarian literature, and Ferenc Verseghy, the poet who rendered the "Marseillaise" into Hungarian. Among the delegates to the various Hungarian Diets were Ferenc Kölcsey, poet, critic, and author of the national anthem; Mihály Vörösmarty, whose poetry and dramas made him the most important writer of Hungarian Romanticism; Mór Jókai, who established the novel as a literary genre in Hungary; Zsigmond Kemény, the master of the historical novel; and Baron József Eötvös, who pioneered the Realistic novel in Hungary and—like some of the other authors mentioned—made Western literature accessible to his compatriots through his translations. Eötvös, who led the Centralist movement in the 1840s, also held positions in two different cabinets. József Bajza, outstanding critic and creator of successful ballads, edited the daily *Kossuth Hírlapja* (Kossuth Journal) during the struggle for freedom. Hungary's greatest narrative poet János Arany espoused the revolutionary cause in some of his verse and worked in Lajos Kossuth's Interior Ministry. Sándor Petőfi, one of the most brilliant Hungarian lyric poets of all times, played a major role in the events of 1848–49. His

"National Song" stirred the enthusiasm of the crowd on March 15, 1848, in Pest, and the demands contained in the "Twelve Points" he had drawn up with Jókai and others became the program of the Revolution. His death on the battlefield made him a martyr in the fight for liberty and a symbol, not only to his nation but abroad as well.

Thus, the political engagement of Imre Madách—holder of various elected county offices; leader of the Centralists in the Nógrád County Assembly; contributor to the *Pesti Hírlap* (Journal of Pest) once edited by Kossuth, but now the voice of the Centralists; and finally member of parliament—seems the rule rather than the exception among Hungarian authors.

The nineteenth century was a period of dramatic changes for all of Europe. The French Revolution and the successful struggle for independence of the former British colonies in America had demonstrated the fragility of political traditions. The established order was increasingly being challenged. The ruling powers clung to their inherited authority, however, and tried to suppress any liberal movement. For most Central Europeans, the end of the Napoleonic era did not bring the constitutional democracy they had hoped for but rather a restoration of the old, absolute systems. The name of Clemens Metternich, Austria's Foreign Minister and later Chancellor, has become permanently attached to this period. The Metternich era was characterized by armed oppression, censorship, a network of paid informers and spies, and an elaborate bureaucracy, all designed to preserve the status quo. But these efforts eventually proved futile. By the time the third quarter of the century was over, the political climate of Europe had changed drastically, and the map of the continent had been redrawn.

Several factors contributed to these changes: The Romantic movement had fostered feelings of nationalism and ethnic pride. The Napoleonic wars had helped reinforce patriotic sentiments. Linguistic and cultural minorities asked for recognition. But ultimately more important were probably social and economic developments: Agricultural societies were transformed into industrial communities, and mechanized manufacturing procedures created a new social class that now also demanded to be acknowledged as a political power. Socialism emerged as an ideology to be reckoned with. Technological advances facilitated communications and travel and aided in the rapid spread of new ideas.

Over the centuries Hungary had held a special position in Europe. Her geographic location made her a buffer between the East and the

West, her language isolated her from all immediate neighbors. Yet Hungarians had been oriented toward the West ever since the tenth century when Géza, the chief of the Magyar tribe, embraced Christianity. His son István, later to be canonized, had asked the Pope to bestow the royal crown of Hungary on him. Despite their willingness to accept the culture of Western Europe, Hungarians, however, had always struggled to maintain their peculiar national character. The long period of Turkish occupation of a major part of the country, terminating only at the end of the seventeenth century, did not succeed in crushing the spirit of a people determined to survive as a nation. Many intellectuals in the early nineteenth century were quite familiar with Johann von Herder's dire warning of 1791 that the Magyars, already outnumbered in their region by other nationalities, might soon disappear without a trace. This awareness strengthened their resistance to the continuing efforts of the Habsburgs to Germanize the country.

The often troublesome association with the Austrian monarchy, ultimately leading to the events of 1848–49, had started in 1526, one of Hungary's darkest years, when the Turks established their rule over Magyar territory in the battle of Mohács. While the majority of the Hungarian nobles constituting the Diet elected János Zápolyai the last native king, supporters of Austria, in a rump Diet, chose Ferdinand of Habsburg to wear the Hungarian crown. Parliamentary assemblies in the seventeenth and eighteenth centuries passed laws accepting the Habsburg dynasty as hereditary kings. But on various occasions Hungarian lawmakers emphasized that their country was not to be regarded as an Austrian possession. The 1791 "Fundamental Laws" declared Hungary a "free kingdom," to be ruled, according to her own laws and customs, by her lawfully crowned hereditary king. The monarch was to convoke the Diet every three years. That principle, however, was soon violated by the next ruler, Franz I, who dissolved the parliamentary assembly in 1812 after its refusal to take over the funding of much of Austria's debt. No Diet was called for another thirteen years.

Hungarian resistance to Austria's efforts for a *Gesamtmonarchie*, a total, unified monarchy, grew during the first half of the century. In 1847 a statement prepared by Ferenc Deák for the liberal opposition in the Lower House of the Diet condemned the prevailing regime as "foreign and non-national" and unconstitutional because it was in violation of the 1791 laws. At the same time Hungary's loyalty to the House of Habsburg was confirmed. On March 3, 1848, Lajos Kossuth addressed the lawmakers and urged passage of an "Address to the Throne" demanding Austrian compliance with the "Oppositional Declaration." This speech is often considered the inauguration of the Revolution. But there was no attempt yet to dissolve the union with Austria. The Vienna government also appeared conciliatory: King Ferdinand V traveled to Pozsony (Bratislava) to sanction the "April Laws" that had been passed by the legislature and that included many of the demands of the "Twelve Points" drafted by Petőfi and the Pest radicals.

These laws provided for some significant changes. The state of the nation was to be that of a limited monarchy with the king exercising his executive powers through a responsible ministry in the twin cities of Buda and Pest. A National Guard was established. The union with Transylvania was enacted, subject to the assent of that region's diet. There were sweeping reforms in the internal political and social structure. The aristocracy, whose representatives made up the Diet, voluntarily gave up century-old privileges. Ever since—in the wake of György Dózsa's peasant rebellion—István Werbőczy's *Tripartitum* of 1514 had codified the rights of Hungarian nobility, the entire peasant class had been condemned to "real and perpetual servitude," and all nobles had been exempted from taxation. Repeated outbreaks of unrest among the disfranchised—most recently prompted by the 1831 cholera epidemic—had shown the explosiveness of the situation. In 1840 the Diet had passed laws giving peasants the right to own land and to buy their freedom. Now the whole institution of serfdom was to be abolished. The Diet had set an important precedent in 1835 by voting to require a toll from everybody, including aristocrats, crossing the suspension bridge between Buda and Pest that Count István Széchenyi had proposed as one of the steps necessary to change Hungary into a modern state. The "April Laws" went much further and called for equal taxation for all. The right to vote was expanded,[1] and freedom of expression and of religion was guaranteed.

As set up by the Diet, the national government under Lajos Batthyány, the country's first Prime Minister, included some of the most outstanding men of the period. The Department of Public Works was in Széchenyi's hands. His 1830 book *Hitel* (Credit) had projected Hungary's path from a backward, feudalistic, agricultural society to a modern industrial nation. Among his many accomplishments were the founding of the Academy of Sciences in 1825 and the establishment of steamship navigation on the Danube. His political opponent Kossuth served as Finance Minister. A gifted journalist and

inspiring orator, Kossuth had strongly disagreed with the evolution-
ary course suggested by Széchenyi whom he, nevertheless, had called
"the greatest Hungarian." Baron Eötvös was given the Ministry of
Religion and Public Education. He, too, had had political differences
with Kossuth who favored utilizing the county unit as an administra-
tive power base, whereas Eötvös and the Centralists were distrustful
of the petty politicking on the regional level and preferred central
concentration of governmental authority. Deák, the great legal mind,
became Minister of Justice.

The apparent peace was quickly shattered. Trouble arose among
Hungary's ethnic minorities. While Magyar politicians, in order to
emphasize cultural autonomy, had demanded that Hungarian be the
country's official language, little attention had been paid to the
claims of Slavic and other nationalities that in official transactions
they, too, were entitled to the use of their native idioms. Austria, although concerned about the growing Pan-Slavic movement, applied
the axiom of *divide et impera* and actively encouraged the nationalistic ambitions of the Rumanians in Transylvania, of the Slovaks, and
especially of the Croats. Croatian troops took advantage of the generally unstable situation and invaded Hungary. The crisis worsened
when Count Franz Lamberg, Austria's Commissioner Extraordinary
with authority over all Croatian and Hungarian troops in the country, was lynched by a Hungarian mob. Batthyány resigned, and the
Diet appointed Kossuth supreme ruler. While the newly established
Honvéd (Home Defense) forces were able to defeat the Croatians,
their clashes with the Imperial Army signaled open warfare between
Austria and Hungary. Ferdinand abdicated in favor of his nephew
Franz Joseph I who did not feel bound by any agreements his prede-
cessor had made. Hungary refused to accept the legality of the resignation. Franz Joseph proclaimed a new Austrian constitution, making
Hungary just one of several provinces of the monarchy. In response,
on April 14, 1848, the Diet in Debrecen declared the country independent.

As Russia came to Austria's assistance, the vastly outnumbered
Hungarian troops had little chance. On August 13 the Hungarian
army surrendered at Világos. Kossuth fled to Turkey. With the fall of
the citadel of Komárom on October 4, the War of Liberation was
over. The victors' revenge was brutal. The Austrian military gov-
ernor had thirteen Hungarian generals hanged. Batthyány was shot,
and the number of executions eventually rose to over a hundred. Almost two thousand people were imprisoned. The military rule was

soon replaced by a civilian administration. This notorious period of absolute Austrian domination became known as the "Bach Era," named after the Habsburg Interior Minister. But all attempts to treat the defeated country as an Austrian colony were increasingly answered by passive resistance and a widespread refusal to pay taxes.[2] Deák was the soul of this resistance.

In 1860 and 1861 Franz Joseph tried to finalize the centralization of the Austrian Empire. His "February Patent" set up a *Reichsrat* (Imperial Council) to include representatives of all provinces of the *Gesamtmonarchie*. A Diet was convoked in Pest (with elections based on the 1848 franchise). Its principal business was to be the nomination of the Hungarian *Reichsrat* delegates. But the parliamentary assembly unanimously refused that assignment, rejecting the "February Patent" as invalid and insisting on the "April Laws" as the only legal basis for the affairs of the country. The only disagreement was about the form of this response to Vienna: the more radical members suggested a Parliamentary Resolution, and the moderates under Deák favored an Address to the Throne, even though Franz Joseph had not been crowned King of Hungary. Deák, opposed to an irrevocable breach with Austria, eventually prevailed and drafted a statement which was courteous in tone but uncompromising in content. The Emperor's response was the dissolution of the Diet. The delegates had also tackled the thorny question of the nationalities, and a committee report, reflecting mainly Eötvös's views, later became the basis of laws dealing with this long neglected problem.

Deák's policy eventually led to an accommodation with Austria. In 1865 Franz Joseph suspended the "February Patent." A year later the union with Transylvania was sanctioned. The Compromise of 1867 established the dual monarchy that was to last another half century. The crowning of Franz Joseph as King of Hungary in June symbolized the demise of the concept of a *Gesamtmonarchie*.

II   Madách's Life: Events and Impacts

Kölcsey wrote what was to become Hungary's national anthem in the year 1823. And the month of January 1823 gave the country two of her greatest poets. Sándor Petőfi was born on the first day of the month, and Imre Madách twenty days later. This coincidence seems symbolic of the societal changes that were to take place in nineteenth-century Hungary: Petőfi, the son of a butcher and a laundress of Slav origin, and Madách, the scion of an old aristocratic family, were both destined to reach the summit of literary fame.

The Madách family belonged to the landed gentry. Their origin can be traced back to the thirteenth century. Since the fifteenth century, the Madáchs had been residing at Alsósztregova (Dolná Strehová) in Nógrád County in Northern Hungary. Among Imre's ancestors were warriors and poets, religious leaders and medical writers, legislators and lawyers, and he seemed to have inherited characteristics of all of them. As early as 1682 there is a record of resistance against the Habsburg dynasty: Péter Madách had a significant role in the Thököly rebellion. During the seventeenth century the family embraced the Lutheran faith, and János, the author's great-grandfather, was actively working for the Protestant cause. Imre's grandfather Sándor converted to Catholicism. He was a very successful lawyer who demonstrated his personal courage when he volunteered to defend the accused in the Martinovics conspiracy trial.

Imre, the poet's father, married Anna Majthényi, a wealthy young woman from another old aristocratic family. Anna was intelligent and strong-willed and had deep religious convictions. She bore her husband five children, two daughters Mari and Anna, and then three sons Imre, Károly, and Pál. When young Imre was only eleven, his father died, leaving Anna Majthényi with the responsibility for rearing the children.

Imre and his brothers and sisters enjoyed the best private education possible. The impact of their French governess can be seen in the occasional French verse Imre wrote for his parents and sisters when only five or six years old. A private tutor, an art instructor, and a dancing teacher provided the children with skills considered essential for members of their class. Family friends, among them university professors and poets, offered additional intellectual stimulation. After having received instruction at home for a few years, Imre briefly attended the Piarist secondary school in Vác. In 1837 he was sent to Pest to complete his education and to earn a university degree. His two brothers went along to attend school in the city.

Imre was a very bright, serious, and sensitive boy, particularly interested in art and reading. His father's extensive library offered him many opportunities to increase his knowledge in literature, philosophy, and history. It is characteristic that even as a child he had the desire to share the fruits of his studies with others. He wrote and edited a weekly journal for the benefit of the members of the Madách household. "Literatúrai kevercs" (Literary Mixture) featured short essays on history, archeology, and other topics.

His constitution was weak, and health problems were to plague him all his life. Perhaps this condition contributed to his early maturity and his seriousness. Fifteen-year-old Imre, writing his mother from Pest, stated his belief that his life would be but a short one.[3] The author's pessimism, often attributed to specific events in his adult life, may in part have resulted from the child's experience of his physical fragility.

Madách's letters give evidence of the strong sense of attachment he always felt for his mother. When, at age seventeen, he published the slim volume of poetry he had written for the girl he loved, the book was dedicated to his mother, not to the "Adeline" of his poems. Years later, when discussing some of the negative characteristics of Eve, the embodiment of womanhood in his drama *Az ember tragédiája (The Tragedy of Man)*, he told Károly Bérczy: "Eve can thank my mother for my not having painted her in more glaring colors." [4]

Madách's friends in Pest included the brothers Albert and Menyhért Lónyay, and Counts Manó and Gyula Andrássy. After the 1867 Compromise, Gyula was to become Hungary's Prime Minister and Menyhért his Minister of Finance and eventually his successor as the head of government. But during their student days in Pest they did not dream of assuming roles of political leadership. Their and their friends' discussions of various topics led to the creation of a little weekly journal, "Mixtura." Madách contributed the poetry for their venture. He also had the pleasure of seeing his first poem printed in a national magazine when *Honművész* (The Homeland Artist) published "Az anya gyermeke sírján" (The Mother at Her Child's Grave).

The twenty-six poems he put together in 1840 under the title *Lantvirágok* (Lyre Blossoms) were the tangible result of an experience that may have had a lasting effect on him. He had fallen in love with Etelka Lónyay, the fourteen-year-old sister of his friends. But Imre and Etelka were too young to think seriously of marriage, and his mother indicated that she would not be happy with a Protestant daughter-in-law. Heartbroken and in poor health, Imre left Pest. After a stay with his sister Mari, to whom he felt particularly close, and a period of convalescence in a fashionable spa, he returned to Alsósztregova to prepare himself for the bar examination.

After the successful completion of his legal studies Madách held several public offices in his native county. He served as Deputy Clerk at the Nógrád County Court at Balassagyarmat and was elected Honorary County Notary. But he was forced to resign after a short time because of a throat ailment. He held the position of County Court Judge and was chosen by the voters as Chief Commissioner with specific responsibility for the military administration on the county level. Once again he had to give up the job for health reasons. His liberal views and his exposure to local and regional politics made him a supporter of Eötvös's Centralists.[5] He assumed a leadership role in this group in the county assembly and reported on the affairs of Nógrád in the *Pesti Hírlap*. His pen name "Timon" is a tribute to French writer Cormenin-Timon whose books he possessed and obviously admired.[6] Other pieces he wrote for the paper give evidence of his liberal and progressive views and his concern about social conditions. He welcomed industrialization because it would benefit the poor peasants and shepherds. His impassioned call for his country to wake up from centuries of sleep is reminiscent of Széchenyi's exhortations to his compatriots.[7]

His contacts with the county's legal community and administration led to new friendships. Most important was his close relationship with Pál Szontágh, who was to be the recipient of some of Madách's most revealing letters, occasionally in poetic form. Pál's wit and irony affected the poet's style, too, and it is not difficult to see Pál as the model for the character of Lucifer in *Az ember tragédiája*. His spirit can also be detected in the satirical epigrams the two friends wrote together with Ferenc Pulszky, who was later to become Kossuth's Minister of Foreign Affairs. Szontágh drew this portrait of Madách for their "Nógrádi képcsarnok" (Nógrád Picture Gallery):

Now you are liberal, you have connections and knowledge,
That's why you are holding your little turned-up nose so high.
Let's wait a little while until you are subprefect in Nógrád,
Your principle will evaporate, and the high nose will remain. (ÖM 2, 1186)

The time from 1843 to 1845 was the period of Madách's greatest artistic productivity. He wrote numerous poems and continued to try his hand at dramatic literature. In 1841 or 1842 his two prose plays *Commodus* and *Nápolyi Endre* (Andrew of Naples) had dealt with history, the latter about a Hungarian prince betrayed by his wife. History was featured again in *Mária királynő* (Queen Mary), and *Csák végnapjai* (Csák's Last Days). Madách would later revise the latter two plays, but they were not published during his lifetime. *Férfi és nő*

(Man and Woman) reinterpreted *The Trachinian Women* of Sophocles. Madách submitted this drama for the 1843 contest of the Hungarian Academy of Sciences, but it met with little enthusiasm. *Csak
tréfa* (Just a Joke) and the fragmentary *Jó név és erény* (Good Reputation and Virtue) dealt with contemporary society. None of these
plays has significant literary merit. They represent well-intended attempts by a gifted but not inspired dilettante. Yet the interest
Madách exhibited in dramatizing historical scenes, and the repeated
examination of the role of woman and the relationship between the
sexes make these works important early studies for *Az ember
tragédiája*. Of the prose tales written during this period and later,
only "A Kolozsiak" (The Kolozsi Family) was published before his
death.

In the winter of 1844–45 Madách met seventeen-year-old Erzsébet
(Erzsi) Fráter, a lively and charming girl. In a letter to Pál Szontágh
he described her impact on him but also showed an awareness of
what was later to destroy their marriage: "Where shall I begin to
write about this microcosm of everything attractive and everything
insidious, of everything good and everything careless, of everything
soulful and everything cynical?" (ÖM 2, 965).

Szontágh, concerned about Erzsi's flirtatious and flighty attitude,
tried in vain to dissuade his friend from a permanent relationship.
Madách's mother also strongly disapproved of her son's intentions.
She had misgivings about Erzsi's character and objected to the fact
that her family was Protestant, not wealthy, and of lesser rank (even
though the Fráters boasted among their ancestors György Mar-
tinuzzi, famous diplomat and cardinal of the sixteenth century). This
time Madách persisted, and in the summer of 1845 they were married. Since Anna Majthényi did not want to live under the same roof
with Erzsi, the newlyweds took up residence at Csesztve, a more remote part of the Madách estate.

The first years of matrimony were happy. But soon the differences
in their temperaments and characters became obvious. The young
bride was moody, shallow, and pleasure-seeking, and she spent
money very freely. She also indicated to her husband that he was not
really capable of fulfilling her needs. Their three surviving children—
their first son had died shortly after birth—Aladár, Jolán, and Borbála
(Barbara, usually called Ára) could not cement a disintegrating marriage.

The national tragedy of 1848–49 also brought personal grief to
Imre Madách. His poor health made his active participation in the

war impossible, but his general attitude and the involvement of his family leave little doubt about his stand. His mother had left for Pest; the poet remained at Csesztve. The letters he received from his brothers and from his mother vividly reflect the excitement of the period. They tell about Kossuth's speeches and Petőfi's fiery appeals, about the establishment of a Hungarian government and the killing of Count Lambert, about the battles against the Austrians, and finally about the fall of Pest.

The war took a heavy toll from the Madách family. Pál, idealistic and patriotic, had taken part in the winter campaign. In April, after Nógrád County had surrendered, Imre tried to persuade him to come home and not risk being hanged for what had become a lost cause. Pál did not heed the advice. When trying to rejoin Kossuth, he contracted pneumonia and died. His sister Mari suffered a horrible death when she, her husband, and their child tried to escape from Transylvania across the border after the armistice. Rumanian bandits murdered them and fed their bodies to the pigs. In his poems "Pál öcsém sírjánál" (At the Grave of My Brother Pál) and "Mária testvérem emlékezete" (Remembrance of My Sister Mária), the poet has eloquently expressed his sorrow. But the final stanza of the elegy for his sister goes beyond his grief and offers a vision of a better future:

> But if the people are ennobled, too,
> If they become human and will be thinking,
> Your spirit will come down again
> To wave their banner, and you will forgive. (ÖM 2, 344)

Long after the surrender at Világos and the bloody Austrian revenge, Madách was to be directly affected by the war. In 1851 he gave shelter to a political fugitive, János Rákóczy, a distant relative who had served as Kossuth's secretary. One of the neighbors probably informed the Austrian authorities. Rákóczy managed to escape, but the poet was arrested. He spent almost a year in prison, first in Pozsony and then in Pest. Allegedly he had to endure beatings during this period.

The failure of the Hungarian fight for freedom and the subsequent era of oppression, the loss of his loved ones, and the degrading experience of his incarceration left a deep impact on the sensitive writer. A further blow was the dissolution of his marriage. While he was imprisoned, Erzsi—despite their precarious financial condition—continued to lead an extravagant life. There were many parties at Csesztve and rumors circulated of her love affairs. When Madách was released from jail but restricted to the city of Pest, she visited him briefly but then returned to Csesztve. Her letter about the serious illness of their daughters and her refusal to call a doctor since "happiness is in the grave anyway" (ÖM 2, 1043) must have been especially tormenting for someone prevented by the authorities from taking care of his family. When he could finally go home, the relationship between the spouses had hopelessly deteriorated. Madách signed Csesztve over to his brother Károly and moved with his family to the old house at Sztregova. The continued frictions between his wife and his mother led to further estrangement. The culmination came in 1854 when Erzsi caused a scandal by attending a dance in the company of another man. Madách insisted on divorce. Jolán stayed with her mother, Ára and Aladár were to live with him. Erzsi's belated attempts at reconciliation were in vain. A few years later Jolán was also taken from her because she was incapable of properly caring for the child.

After the divorce Madách withdrew more and more. He spent much of his time in a remote room of the house and seldom had contact even with his children or his mother. The man who had always enjoyed the companionship of his friends now earned the nickname of the "Recluse of Sztregova." His letters to Szontágh from this period show the depth of his gloom.[8] But he took up writing again, and out of his bitter experiences grew some of his best poems. He took the Bach regime to task in his "Aristophanic" comedy *A civilizátor* (The Civilizer) of 1859. And between February 17, 1859, and March 26, 1860, he wrote his masterpiece *Az ember tragédiája*. It is impossible to say exactly when he had conceived the idea to depict the history of mankind in a Faustian drama. There are indications that some of the thoughts that took definite shape in his play had been on his mind for years.

It is as if the work on this dramatic poem had also contributed to Madách's decision to break out of his self-imposed seclusion. He won election as the representative of Balassagyarmat at the 1861 Diet in Pest. His parliamentary speeches reveal him as an eloquent opponent of the *Gesamtmonarchie*, as a firm believer in the goals of 1848, and as concerned about the problem of the nationalities. A contemporary observer described his appearance and impact:

One of the most striking figures in the House of Representatives is Imre Madách. Blond hair, a Slavic profile, a drooping mustache in the manner of the Chinese, but a breast harboring Hungarian feelings, and a mind nurtured on European culture. His eloquence is not of a flaming nature, it is a quiet fire, crackling occasionally, and then surprising his laughing audience with the flare of a striking idea or of a completely new redolent phrasing of a drastic but by no means unpleasant image. Whoever has read his speeches will have sensed the difference between him and the mere phrasemongers; his images are definitely not labored but rather the most natural vehicle of his ideas. His figures of speech are not empty but rather contain a healthy thought.[9]

Madách had taken the manuscript of his play to Pest; Szontágh had suggested showing it to János Arany, considered the greatest contemporary literary authority. Arany's initial reaction was negative. After glancing at the first scene, he put the work aside as a rather inferior imitation of Goethe's *Faust*. But Madách felt that his drama was worthy of serious consideration. When he did not hear from Arany, he asked the poet Pál Jámbor to remind the great man of his promise to evaluate the poem.

Perhaps Madách's growing reputation as a gifted parliamentary speaker also caused Arany to take a second look at the play. In the summer of 1861 he completed his perusal of the poem, and his initial disappointment had changed to enthusiasm. On August 25 he wrote to Mihály Tompa that he had discovered a "genuine talent." He called *Az ember tragédiája* a "*Faust*-like composition, but standing completely on its own feet." He praised the "grand ideas" it contained and viewed Madách as "the first talent after Petőfi to exhibit a completely individual orientation." [10] On September 12 Madách received the letter he had been waiting for. Arany termed the tragedy "an excellent work, both in conception and in composition" (ÖM 2, 1001). He pointed to certain flaws in the poetic language but offered his assistance in smoothing out awkward passages if the author agreed. Madách eagerly accepted.

When Arany read the first four scenes to the Kisfaludy Society on October 30, they were received with tremendous applause. The Society published the play on January 16, 1862. A second edition appeared in 1863, a third one in 1869. Two weeks after the publication of *Az ember tragédiája* its author was elected to the Kisfaludy Society. In 1863 he became a corresponding member of the Academy of Sciences.

Madách could not repeat the overwhelming success of this drama. He rewrote *Csák végnapjai* (Csák's Last Days) and submitted his *Mózes* (Moses), written immediately after the completion of *Az ember*

tragédiája, for the 1861 Academy contest, but the play failed to win
more than an honorable mention and the judges called the biblical
drama a "dramatized epic."

The poet could not complete his last play, *Tündérálom* (Fairy
Dream), a phantasy reminiscent of Vörösmarty's *Csongor és Tünde*
and Shakespeare's *Midsummer Night's Dream.* His health, further
weakened through his incarceration, deteriorated rapidly. An acute
heart ailment prevented him from reading his inaugural speech at the
Academy in the spring of 1864. Károly Bérczy had to share Madách's
essay "A nőről, különösen aesthetikai szempontból" (On Woman,
Particularly from an Esthetic Point of View) with the Academicians.

On October 5, 1864, Imre Madách died at Alsósztregova. One of
his eulogists said of him: "Wherever sacrifices had to be made, the
deceased made sacrifices; wherever it was necessary to fight, he
fought; wherever it was possible to speak freely, he spoke; and wherever he had to risk his life, he took that risk. He was, in a word, a
diamond, sparkling at all times regardless from which side one might
look." [11]

III   *Madách's Cultural World: Hungary and Europe*

Wolfgang Margendorff has called *Az ember tragédiája* a creation of
"Magyar culture that had become European." [12] To some extent this
assessment is accurate, especially when one compares—as he did—
Madách's work with the two outstanding examples of Hungarian dramatic writing preceding it, József Katona's *Bánk bán* (Ban Bank) and
Mihály Vörösmarty's *Csongor és Tünde,* (Csongor and Tünde), both of
which were clearly directed at Hungarian audiences. In contrast,
Madách's play contains few specific Hungarian references—at least
on the surface—and has a far more universal appeal.

Yet Margendorff's statement is somewhat misleading. Tradition-
ally, the outlook of Hungarian culture had been European. Magyar
poets had accepted as binding the metrical and structural rules developed in the West even though their own idiom might have called for
different approaches. Hungarian men of letters of the eighteenth and
nineteenth centuries viewed themselves very much as part of European culture. They were familiar with world literature and with classical and contemporary Western thought.

Imre Madách exemplifies this cosmopolitan attitude. At the age of
five he was already learning to read and write not only his native

tongue but also German, French, and Latin (then still the official government language). His correspondence and his notes indicate his familiarity with those languages and the cultures they represent. This linguistic preparation also gave him access to the extensive library in his parental home.

A large part of that book collection dated back to Sándor, the poet's grandfather, whose son had further augmented it. Imre Madách himself purchased additional volumes. There were probably up to fifteen hundred titles in his library. Of these, 1084 have been identified. But the playwright's familiarity with additional authors can be deduced from his notes and letters and from evidence in his works.

Many of the legal and theological or philosophical texts reflect Sándor's interests. He emerges as a typical representative of the Enlightenment. Besides books by Martin Luther and Thomas à Kempis, he acquired volumes by Immanuel Kant and Moses Mendelssohn, and German translations of works by Jean-Jacques Rousseau and Thomas Paine. An extensive collection on Freemasonry and on the secret society of the Illuminati attests to one of his preoccupations. He also displayed an obvious interest in Hungarian history but did not pay much attention to Magyar literature.

Sándor's son Imre was not quite his father's equal in terms of intellectual depth. But he and his well-educated wife, who was interested in many facets of culture, added greater breadth to the book holdings. Works by Károly Kisfaludy and András Dugonics indicate an awareness of native literature. Imre's Francophile attitude is obvious from the number of French authors he added. He purchased tomes by Jean Baptiste Molière, François de Salignac de la Mothe Fénélon, Jean de LaFontaine, François Marie Arouet Voltaire, and others. His father's library had featured German and Latin texts almost exclusively, but Imre bought books written in French as well. His interest in history, particularly in the era of Napoleon, is clear from his collection of nonfiction volumes.

The playwright himself acquired many outstanding works of world literature. Complete editions of Goethe and Schiller were added, along with German translations of Shakespeare and Byron. Madách read Victor Hugo and other French Romanticists as well as some of the poetry of Heinrich Heine. Increasingly, Hungarian names appear among the authors he included: János Arany, József Bajza, Gábor Dayka, Károly and Sándor Kisfaludy, Ferenc Kölcsey, Ede Szigligeti,

and Mihály Vörösmarty. Yet by the time he died only a comparatively small fraction of the volumes in his library had been written by
Hungarians: there were sixty-one Magyar writers, as compared with
sixty-four Latin authors, eighty-six Frenchmen, 160 Englishmen, and
357 Germans. A breakdown according to languages emphasizes the
strong impact of German culture even more: 741 of the volumes were
in German, 118 in Hungarian, 115 in French, and sixty-nine in Latin.
Not only were the works of John Milton and Edward Young accessible to him only in German translations, but also the Koran and the
Arabian Nights, Dante's *Divine Comedy* and Voltaire's *Candide*.
Even some of his books by Hungarians were in German.

Madách's reading was not limited to literature. Alexander von
Humboldt's *Cosmos* and other titles show his interest in the natural
sciences. He was familiar with Georg Wilhelm Friedrich Hegel's philosophy of history, and he owned Ludwig Feuerbach's *Essence of
Christianity*. Plato's *Republic* and Charles Fourier's utopian ideas left
traces in his work. He was interested in French political writers, but
his library also gives evidence of his attention to national politics. He
owned Széchenyi's *Hitel* (Credit) and Hungarian and German versions of Count József Dessewffy's discussion of the book. Széchenyi's
response to Kossuth, a German translation of his 1842 report on the
Hungarian Academy of Sciences, Imre Vachot's *Országgyűlési al-
manach* (Diet Almanac), and a German title of 1846, *Geschichtliche
Fragmente und das ungarische Staatsleben neuerer Zeit* (Historic
Fragments and Hungarian Public Life of Recent Times) are among a
number of publications reflecting Hungarian politics before 1848.

The presence of these latter titles in his library is significant. While
Madách was familiar with the literature and thought of Western Europe, from the classical works of Greece and Rome to the major (and
some of the minor) writers of Britain, France, and Germany, he also
grew up during a period of increasing Hungarian cultural autonomy.
He was aware of the efforts of Ferenc Kazinczy—one of the men de-
fended by his grandfather—to create a Hungarian literary language
capable of expressing nuances of thought and feeling. Kazinczy had
fought the extreme striving for originality and ethnic purity exhibited
by the more conservative circle of provincial nobles around Sándor
Kisfaludy. Instead, he used German Classicism, especially Goethe's
works, as a model, just as in the area of economics Széchenyi looked
at more advanced industrialized societies abroad in an effort to make
his own nation more autonomous.

Széchenyi had also made a major contribution to the increasing emphasis on the Hungarian language. He had caused quite a stir when he first addressed the Diet in his native language instead of the traditional Latin. In 1843 Hungarian finally became the country's official language. When Madách attended the university in Pest, professors were beginning to lecture in Hungarian. The Academy of Sciences fostered an awareness of Magyar culture in the 1830s. Similarly, the Kisfaludy Society—founded in 1836 to cultivate the memory of Károly Kisfaludy who had greatly contributed to the creation of a native literature—stressed the national trend in Hungarian writing. Authors like Vörösmarty, Bajza, and Ferenc Toldy enthusiastically followed Károly Kisfaludy's example and later gave valuable support to promising young poets such as Petőfi and Arany. Guidance was provided by publications like *Tudományos Gyüjtemény* (Scientific Collection), *Athenaeum*,[13] and the yearbook *Aurora*.[14] Another important factor was the opening of the National Theater in Pest in 1837. Not until the beginning of the century had Pest seen regular performances of plays in Hungarian, but they had still been subordinated to the German theater company. Now there was an institution that offered new opportunities to actors and—of equal importance—to Hungarian dramatic writers.

Health problems prevented Madách from frequenting the National Theater during his student days. But it is hardly accidental that he penned his first dramatic scenes during those years. It is also worth noting that he often selected topics from Hungarian history for his plays, such as *Mária királynő* (Queen Mary), *Csák végnapjai* (Csák's Last Days), *Nápolyi Endre* (Andrew of Naples), and the 1855 fragment *II. Lajos* (Lajos II). His notes show that he considered other historical subjects: *Verbőczy*—for which a biography in his library had furnished information—*Atilla fiai* (Attila's Sons), and *András és Borics* (Andrew and Borics) remained unwritten. But even some works that seem unrelated to Hungarian culture have actually been shaped by it. His last drama fragment *Tündérálom* takes its title from a Petőfi poem in which the "fairy dream" serves as an allegorical lyric biography. The specific reference to Petőfi's *János Vitéz* (János the Hero, or Sir János) in *Tündérálom* (ÖM 1, 1060) supports the thesis that the identical title is no coincidence but was chosen to honor a great poet and patriot. Thematically, much of Madách's lyrical poetry is also closely tied to the culture of his native land, to its history, and to its scenery.

Thus, we find in Madách's cultural background—and reflected in his writings, especially in *Az ember tragédiája*—a unique blend of European and Magyar elements. It is this combination that makes his work accessible to an international audience while Hungarians can see it as representative of their national experience.

CHAPTER 2

From the First Blossoms of a Lyre
to a Fairy Dream:
Madách's Development as a Writer

I Romanticism and Reality: Madách's Poetry

IMRE Madách made his literary debut as a lyrical poet, not as a dramatist. He was only sixteen years old when a respected journal published "Az anya gyermeke sírján." While not a masterpiece, the poem in which a bereaved mother expresses her pain and bitterness to a silent God is remarkably mature. The first and last stanzas form an effective frame in their near-identity, and the simplicity of the language and the handling of the rhymes are reminiscent of folk poetry. The patriotic note, to become characteristic of much of Madách's work, is already sounded in this first attempt: the mother has taught her child to regard the homeland as a "second mother," to defend its cause, to extol its sons and convert its enemies (ÖM 2, 847).

A year later the same tendency to appeal to patriotic feelings resulted in the young poet's first problems with censorship when he had his slim verse collection *Lantvirágok* (Lyre Blossoms) printed. Many of the twenty-six poems deal with love, longing, and resignation, and some of these "blossoms of a lyre" reflect a fashionable sentiment of *Weltschmerz*. The influence of Bajza can be detected in this Romantic collection, but the poems voicing devotion to Hungary and a yearning for freedom are reminiscent of Kölcsey. The censor objected to one of the poems on religious grounds and to two others for political reasons. "Hős nő" (Heroic Woman), in which the heroine bemoaned the treacherous execution of the rebellious István Kont by King Zsigmond, had to be rewritten as "Mohács terén" (On the Battlefield of Mohács) about Boris who has fallen in the fight against the Turks. Similarly, in "Róma" (Rome) Lucretia is now mourning the lost freedom of Rome, not Anna that of Hungary. Neither poem was particularly revolutionary in its original form. In 1830 Vörösmarty had written a play about Kont's rebellion and execution which may have provided a stimulus for "Hős nő" since the impact of Vörösmarty on Madách's lyrical work in general is quite pronounced. But in being forced to change what he had written, the young Romanticist for the first time came face to face with the reality of the political situation.

After *Lantvirágok*, Madách saw only ten more of his poems in print. The bulk of his lyrical production, arranged by him for possible publication toward the end of his life, became known only after his death. His original drafts are not preserved, and his arrangement was not chronological but rather according to themes, moods, and genres. As a result, the debate over his creative method and especially over the dates of origin of many of the poems has been going on for more than a century. In some cases clear or veiled references to biographical or historical facts aid in the determination of the chronology, but often there is no such clue. Scholars have also disagreed over the artistic merits of Madách's lyrical works. Most critics see him essentially as a dramatist who only occasionally succeeded in writing poetry of lasting importance. But sometimes, as in the assessment of László Bóka, his poetic talent is seen as primarily lyrical.[1] Yet it seems obvious that Madách's fame and significance lie in his philosophic drama. Without *Az ember tragédiája*, it is not likely that the lyricist Madách would have attracted much critical attention. As it stands, some of his poems are rightly regarded as important preliminary studies for his play, and others are valued for the insight they give into the writer's soul. As a record of his emotional reactions to events in his own life and in the life of the nation, they add up to a remarkable interior autobiography.

The love poems in *Lantvirágok*, inspired by Madách's feelings for Etelka Lónyay, reflected a Romantic view of love and the tendency to go from personal experience to more general concepts. The Romantic glorification of love as a universal force holding the world together is still quite clear in the "Vadrózsák" (Wild Roses) cycle, probably written in 1845 and dedicated to Erzsi. The thought already expressed in his play *Commodus* is now stated most strikingly: "The sacred chain of love is the universe,/ And in it, we, too, are a tiny particle" (ÖM 2, 40). The lover becomes part of this eternal force. The initial period of marital bliss led to poems expressing the fulfillment of love and the quiet happiness of domestic life in the style of Petőfi rather than Vörösmarty. Károly Horváth claims that the impact of Petőfi's "Megunt rabság" (Weary of Imprisonment) of 1844 can be shown in each verse of "Boldogság és szenvedély" (Happiness and Passion).[2] The experiences of 1848–49 and the Bach period and of the failure of his marriage were again translated into a bitter and pessimistic world view as it emerges in poems like "Egy vetélytárshoz" (To a Rival) or "P. barátomhoz" (To My Friend P.), a poetic epistle addressed to Pál Szontágh in 1857. Madách's grief over the brutal loss of his brother and sister was transformed into poetry, and the short but eloquent epitaphs "Petőfi sírján" (At Petőfi's Grave) and "Az aradi sírra" (For the Grave of Arad) show how deeply he was affected by the death of the brilliant lyricist and by the Austrian execution of the Hungarian freedom fighters.

Madách's commitment to the cause of liberty was unconditional. "Költő és szabadság" (The Poet and Freedom) speaks in epigrammatic conciseness about this engagement. He violently opposed the willingness of some of his compatriots to accept a compromise with Austria after the war. "Csak béke, béke" (Only Peace, Peace) castigates those who are already negotiating peace while the graves of the heroes fallen for freedom are still bare and wounds are still bleeding. His indignation over the faint-heartedness of those who do not realize that the "peace" they desire is death becomes a statement of general philosophy that will be expressed in very similar terms in *Az ember tragédiája:* "Life is struggle, rest is death;/ Even if there is a thunderstorm in the summer sky,/ What are you afraid of?" (ÖM 2, 328). "Síri dal" (Grave Song) vows in Petőfi's spirit the continuation of the war of liberation as the fight against despotism. From the struggle for Magyar liberty will spring the fight for world freedom.

Much of Madách's patriotic poetry—as well as his love and nature poems—is Romantic in spirit. But some of the works inspired by the war, such as the miniatures of military life in the cycle "Tábori képek" (Camp Images), are unsentimental and do not idealize the real world. In some other examples the poet, in describing landscapes or scenes from everyday life, emerges as a lyrical Realist. "Ősszel" (In Autumn) offers an idyllic but factual description of a rural estate and its denizens in their normal activities. "Alföldi utazás" (Traveling in the Great Plains) contains some stanzas that skillfully sketch the landscape of the region. "Egy nyíri temetőn" (In a Cemetery in the Nyír District), probably written in 1845, starts with a strikingly modern depiction of the desolate scenery with its bleak sand, hill next to hill like a field of graves; a stagnant pond below; and above, dressed in white, lonely birches rising up. The wailing of the lapwings, the booming cry of the bitterns, and the ripple of the feather grass around the cemetery are all features of the "poetry of bleakness," as István Sőtér phrased it.[3] But—as in several other poems—this tone is not sustained throughout: the powerful images of reality soon give way to abstract thoughts and philosophical generalizations.

One of Madách's most successful lyrical creations is "Dalforrás" (Fountain of Song) which shows the influence of Petőfi's "Dalaim" (My Songs) although the message is quite different. In his poetry—as in his dramatic works—Madách made no attempt to hide the inspirations that had come from others, probably because he was sure of his basic originality of thought and emotion. "Dalforrás" seems to reflect the short time in the poet's life when he had found peace with himself and the world. It blends the Romantic longing for harmony with nature, pantheistic ideas, and patriotic feelings in a unique way, and its use of language and form is skillful. The middle of each stanza has the refrain-like repetition of the phrase, "I do not even know how far my soul reaches" and the expression of the sensation of unity with "the sun's light," "dawn," "the quiet night," "the mist of the pale autumn," and "the clouds of tempest" (ÖM 2, 299–301). Surprisingly, the conscious interruption of this evocation of harmony between man and nature through the introduction of the theme of love of country does not seem inappropriate.

Many of Madách's philosophical poems touch on ideas and themes that later find their ultimate expression in *Az ember tragédiája.* "A nő teremtése" (The Creation of Woman) presents Lucifer as the rebel, and "Az első halott" (The First Death) deals with man's early sinfulness and outlines the function of womanhood that the Lord later describes to Eve at the end of Madách's drama. A recurring theme in these poems is the loss of the original harmony, and man's isolation and alienation. In "Ó- és újkor" (Old and New Times) the poet follows the example of Kölcsey and Arany in contrasting the world of harmony and joy of classical Greece with later times that brought only pain and unrest to humanity. But usually there is no such clear reference to a specific idealized period in history. It is the loss of Paradise, the loss of the original unity with God and nature that is mourned in the longer of the two poems with the identical title "Hit és tudás" (Faith and Knowledge). Neither God's concern nor man's hope can cross the great void that came into being when the circle of the universe was broken in which God and man had lived together (ÖM 2, 302). The pantheistic desire for harmony is again expressed in "Gyermekimhez" (For My Children). The message of Eden is still in the souls of children, and "star and blade of grass, animal and the child's heart" can understand it. But man in his pride has separated himself and is foolishly putting his trust in himself only. Thus he does

not understand that message anymore, and the world for him becomes sad and silent (ÖM 2, 345). This theme of man's loneliness is
treated over and over, whether in the image of the wanderer in exile
who is alienated from his surroundings in "Önvád" (Self-Reproach),
or in the look at history of "Éjféli gondolatok" (Thoughts at Mid-
night) which illustrates the inability of man to find his proper place.
The condemnation of the masses, created "for the yoke" and willing
to crucify their Savior and kiss the tyrant's whip (ÖM 2, 324), will
recur in *Az ember tragédiája* and in Madách's Moses drama.

Madách's poetry as a whole reflects a sensitive and thoughtful author, aware of the literary trends of his period but searching for his
own mode of expression; a man occasionally savoring joy and con-
tentment but often given to gloomy despair; a patriot never wavering
in his commitment to the cause of national freedom but deeply
grieved by the events of his times; an individualist with the tendency
to generalize from his personal experience; a Romanticist looking at
reality; a lyricist on his way to writing a dramatic masterpiece.

II   *The Frustrated Storyteller: Madách's Prose Narratives*

Critics seem to agree that Madách's five prose tales represent the
least successful aspect of his literary production. Characteristically,
Sőtér neither discusses them in his Madách monograph nor does he
include any in his edition of the poet's selected works.[4] They are
marred by complicated and sometimes unclear plots and melodramatic effects, by poorly developed and unbelievable characters, and
by a graceless prose style. There is surprisingly little evidence of artistic growth between "Duló Zebedeus kalandjai" (Zebedee Duló's Adventures) of 1842 and "A Kolozsiak" (The Kolozsi Family) of 1864,
and the contrast between his narrative prose and his eloquent
speeches is particularly striking.

"Duló Zebedeus kalandjai" is the humorous account of the first-
person narrator's misadventures during a visit to Pest in an attempt to
find a wife. The influence of Károly Kisfaludy's comic short stories is
evident. The one remarkable feature might be the satiric portrayal of
the country gentleman which precedes by three years Petőfi's similar
description in his famous poem "A magyar nemes" (The Hungarian
Nobleman): Duló reflects about his preference for dogs over human
beings because animals do not try to rise above their station, rejects
the idea of reading as books are only for those who need to learn—and
he, after all, is a gentleman—and expresses his satisfaction with the

reaction of his servants when he gives orders and with the humbleness of the village people who have to greet him (ÖM 2, 400).

"Az ecce homo" (The Ecce Homo) seems intended as an illustration of Rousseau's philosophy. Spiridion has grown up in the Javanese jungle and is taken to Europe to face the corruption of seventeenth-century society, dominated by the Church. The abundance of melodramatic elements makes the story almost a parody of popular Romantic tales. There are the evil monk, scheming to have various people murdered so that their possessions will fall to the Church; the terror of the Inquisition; the rescue of the condemned from the burning stake; insanity; escape from a convent; incest; the murder of mother and infant by a conspiring physician; and the union in death of two half brothers who had become mortal enemies. By using the past as the setting for this story, Madách may again have followed Kisfaludy who chose contemporary backgrounds only for his humorous tales.

"Krónika két pénzdarab sorsáról" (Chronicle of the Fate of Two Coins) is another Romantic story that is rich in improbable twists. But it reflects the social consciousness of young Madách. Aristocrats and rich people are depicted as the villains, and the poor appear as the victims of society and its unjust laws: Viola is driven into prostitution; Pista, her honest young lover, is sent to prison despite his innocence and later becomes a beggar after having lost his leg in the war.

"Hétköznapi történet" (Everyday Story) challenges society's condemnation of the "fallen woman" and presents in Júlia the emancipated female who finds an understanding and honest man whose devoted and faithful wife she becomes. Madách did not date this story, obviously written in the 1840s, and Károly Horváth's suggestion that it might reflect the impact of the poet's first encounter with Erzsi Fráter is not without merit.[5]

"A Kolozsiak" is the story of a woman's elaborate plans to avenge her husband's murder, committed by her brother-in-law. In carrying out her scheme, she unwittingly abducts her own daughter whom she had believed to be dead, and eventually causes the girl's death along with that of Márk Kolozsi, the target of her revenge. The story is set in the seventeenth century following Thököly's *kuruc* uprising, but Madách makes little effort to sketch out the rich historic background.

It is obvious that Madách's imagination and his strong emotional reactions to his world did not find the appropriate medium in the prose narrative. While Kisfaludy was able to write successful short stories and to excel as a dramatist, the playwright Madách remained a frustrated storyteller.

III   *The Making of a Dramatist: Madách's Earlier Works*

In evaluating Madách's first dramatic attempts, it should be remembered that he was between seventeen and nineteen years old when he wrote *Commodus* and *Nápolyi Endre* (Andrew of Naples).[6] He knew little about the theater, and Hungarian drama did not have enough of a tradition to give him much guidance.

It seems only natural for a beginning playwright to turn to historical themes supplying ready-made plots and characters. The atmosphere of decadent Rome and the poisoning of Emperor Commodus by his mistress Marcia in 192 A.D. provided the material for the four acts of Madách's prose drama which he apparently intended to rewrite later in iambic verse. Elements of Romantic horror fiction abound: the abduction of an innocent young woman by a depraved and powerful man; the mother who becomes insane in her grief; one brother's self-sacrifice for his sibling and their exchange of clothing to facilitate a prison escape; and the depiction of Christians facing death in the arena. There are shortcomings in plot and character development; some of the dialogue is awkward; but Madách already demonstrates one skill that points forward to *Az ember tragédiája:* he manages to paint a convincing picture of an historical period.

Madách's estate contained his notes for *Commodus* and for most of his other dramas. They offer an interesting insight into his approach. Rather than outlining action, he gives character sketches of the principal figures and jots down thoughts and snatches of dialogue. This is the description of the title hero: "He assumes the throne through sin, wants to immerse himself completely in lust, but nothing excites him anymore, the kiss is cold, laughter is rare. The bad deed is the permanent key to his soul. He loves his life and dreads his death" (ÖM 2, 713). The play then attempts to flesh out and illustrate this summary. More often than not, Madách's characters are personifications of his ideas rather than psychologically convincing portraits of real people.

While *Commodus*—and the *Brutus* planned by Madách—and the theme of tyrannicide may have some indirect connection with Hungarian history, *Nápolyi Endre* is the first of several dramas to deal directly with events in the nation's past. In the five-act prose play Madách also introduces a theme that will occur again and again in his work: the relationship between the sexes. The story of the assassination of the Hungarian Anjou prince Endre in 1345, most likely arranged by his wife Queen Johanna of Naples, gave Madách the opportunity to portray the clash of two cultures and to use again some of the Romantic elements of *Commodus*. The figures of the monk Robert as one of the conspirators and of Cabanis, the assassin who kills his own daughter by mistake, are popular contemporary stereotypes. Madách's lack of dramaturgical experience and his weakness in presenting believable characters and effective dialogue are as obvious as are his problems in combining the factual account of Ignác Aurél Fessler's comprehensive work on Hungarian history with the internal logic flowing from the action of a stage play. In the second act the visit of Endre's mother from Hungary, to convince her son to leave the hostile surroundings, is an historic event; but after her mission fails, she simply drops out of the drama. Shortly before Endre's murder, Durazzo, one of the conspirators, has a completely unmotivated and unexplained change of heart. Yet even this immature work—influenced, as his other plays of the time, by Victor Hugo, Schiller, and Shakespeare—shows promise and is an important first step toward the achievement to come almost two decades later. Madách did not revise *Nápolyi Endre*, but according to his notes he wanted to use parts of it for a play on the thematically related story of Samson and Delilah.

Fourteenth-century history again provides the background for *Mária királynő* (Queen Mary) and *Csák végnapjai* (Csák's Last Days). The two plays of 1843 depict Magyar resistance to foreign-born rulers; both deal with the question of female succession to the throne of Hungary; both combine historic facts with poetic invention but suffer from the same inadequate fusion of these elements as did *Nápolyi Endre*. Romantic subplots interfere with the effective presentation of important events in the nation's history. Inconsistencies in plot development and characterization and uneven poetic language reveal the twenty-year-old amateur with little theater experience.

Mária királynő is based on the fighting over the Hungarian crown in the period between the death of Lajos I in 1382 and the coronation of Zsigmond, Queen Mária's husband, in 1387. The murder of King Károly III of Anjou is one of the central incidents. The malcontents under Palizsnay rise up against the "petticoat rule" of the queen but have to concede defeat when Zsigmond becomes Hungary's king and Mária can take her place next to him on the throne. Her tragic love for her cupbearer Forgách could have led to a dramatic conflict between passion and duty in her soul, but this motif is not adequately developed. Forgách is eventually stabbed by Palizsnay who inexplicably has fallen in love with his prisoner Mária. The Venetian intervention that frees the queen is based on the historical account but appears as the *deus ex machina* in Madách's Romantic drama.

Only the 1855 revised version exists of *Mária királynő*. In the case of *Csák végnapjai*, we have an opportunity to compare the original play with the rather hastily prepared revision of 1861. Máté Csák, one of the two great territorial magnates whose forces were defeated in the battle of Rozgony in 1312 by Róbert Károly, the first Hungarian Anjou king, is trying to save the crown for the native Árpád dynasty. But when Erzsébet, the daughter of the last Árpád king, decides to enter a convent because she does not want any more bloodshed, Csák gives up the struggle that has become meaningless. The subplot of Dávid Omode's passionate love for Erzsébet detracts from the play's unity by obscuring her motivation for escaping into the peace of the convent. The transformation of the notorious oligarch Csák into a fighter for national independence and legitimacy—emphasized in the drama through the hero's self-identification with Brutus—had been pioneered by Károly Kisfaludy whose dramatic fragment *Csák Máté* had first been published in 1831 and obviously influenced Madách's conception of Csák's character.

The 1861 version features some cuts and reorganized scenes and certain improvements in the language but retains the inconsistencies and structural weaknesses of the original draft. When Arany, after reading the revised manuscript, suggested that Madách not publish it until *Az ember tragédiája* had appeared in print, the sensitive playwright had to be persuaded not to burn the drama. He had obviously rewritten it because of its topicality, and both Voinovich and Sőtér point to the parallels between Csák's fight for the cause of the nation and the events of 1848–49 and the contemporary Hungarian opposition to Austria's attempts to incorporate the country into the *Gesamtmonarchie.*[7] In this view, a character like Zách, who supports the foreign-born king, represents those Magyar politicians who favored a compromise with Austria, a position that Madách strongly opposed. It should be kept in mind, however, that most of the passages inviting such interpretation were already part of the 1843 play. Thus, in the light of the political situation, the drama assumed a new meaning beyond its author's original intention.

In *Férfi és nő* (Man and Woman), although written during the same period as these historical plays, Madách turned from his nation's past to Greek myth, and from Kisfaludy to Sophocles. In his fragmentary essay of 1842, "Művészeti értekezés" (Discourse on Art), he had tried to develop a dramatic theory based on his study of the works of the Greek playwright. Now he selected the theme of Heracles between Deianeira and Iola, featured in *The Trachinian Women*. But his emphasis is quite different. Sophocles had concentrated on Deianeira and written a drama on the psychology of jealousy. Madách, in accord with European literary tendencies of the time, made Heracles the center of action and drew the portrait of a Romantic titan. His hero is torn between human love that threatens to tie him to earth and divine aspirations that are part of his dual nature. The tragedy is not brought about by man's unfaithfulness and disregard for established morality; Madách rather concentrates on the great man who is not understood by women. Only in death, which he freely chooses, is Heracles united with Hebe, the goddess of youth. Madách, the young poet, seems to say that man can achieve greatness only without woman and her ties to the material world. The mature playwright will later show that only with woman can man reach his goal: Adam and Eve belong together and complement each other. Yet the tendency to translate personal experiences and beliefs into generalized concepts emerges even in this youthful drama. While Heracles does not yet represent humanity, Madách makes him the prototype of maleness as he sees it.

The relationship between the sexes is also a prominent theme in his two social dramas. Only the first act of *Jó név és erény* (Good Reputation and Virtue) was completed, but the author's outline introduces the heroine as a woman of lower social rank who marries an aristocrat in order to elevate her status, then has him killed by her lover, and finally becomes insane when her fading youth and beauty cause her companion's passions to cool. Perhaps Madách did not complete the work because he was aware of the immaturity it reflected, but it is interesting to see how motifs from *Commodus* and *Nápolyi Endre* were transplanted into the Hungarian society of the 1830s and how there is almost a premonition of the type of woman whom he would meet and marry a short time later.

Csak tréfa (Just a Joke) is more important, especially as an insight into the reactions of the young writer to the society he encountered at Balassagyarmat. The devastating view of corruption in the administration of justice, the political opportunism and dishonesty, and the approach to matrimony based on economic considerations rather than love reflect personal observations. It is the poet himself who speaks through his hero, the idealistic politician Zordy who is destroyed through the manipulations of a powerful and scheming woman.[8] Characteristically, Madách's experiences in Nógrád County are transformed into a view of the world. Zordy's tragedy is the recurring theme of the misunderstood and betrayed visionary. Jolán is the female who is too weak to follow her heart and instead enters a marriage of convenience. But in the singer Bianka the prototype of the emancipated woman emerges for the first time in Madách's dramatic work. Unfortunately, the play is marred by too many weaknesses to make its social criticism effective, and the impact of what could have been a precursor of Ibsen's portrayal of societal corruption is further blunted by Madách's selection of verse instead of prose.

Form and intent blend well, however, in his last drama before *Az ember tragédiája*. He called *A civilizátor* "a comedy in the manner of Aristophanes," and it is indeed carefully modeled after the works of the great satirist. The political burlesque ridicules the despised Bach regime just as Aristophanes had exposed the vices and follies of his time to the laughter of the Athenians. Madách imitates the strophe and antistrophe of the Greek chorus; and where Aristophanes had used birds, frogs, and wasps to provide the comments in his plays, the Hungarian satire features a chorus of cockroaches. This choice is ingenious. Not only does this insect elicit an immediate emotional response, but the Hungarian word for it, *svábbogár*, literally translates as "Swabian bug," and the German settlers in Hungary were generally called "Swabians" regardless of their specific origin.

Stroom, the "great civilizer" as he refers to himself, has come to bring "Germanic-Christian culture" to the Hungarian barbarians. He incites the servants of Uncle István, the small landholder representing the Hungarian people, to participate in the overthrow of their master. István is thrown out of his house where Stroom, assisted by his army of cockroaches and mouthing Hegelian slogans, establishes a bureaucratic regime. But István's former servants, symbolizing the ethnic minorities of the country, soon realize that their situation has changed for the worse. They join their old master in chasing out the civilizer and his vermin associates. As a sad organ-grinder, Stroom sings about his failed mission: "My idea was glorious, proud, outstanding:/ The unified strong monarchy" (ÖM 1, 507).

While Madách's comedy with its sometimes forced humor is no literary masterpiece, it is significant as a successful evocation of the spirit of Aristophanes. And it is an important political statement by a man soon to be elected to represent his community in the national Diet.

IV   *Descent from the Summit: Madách's Last Plays*

Madách's first dramatic attempts dealing with conflicts among individuals were based in part on history or mythology. With *A civilizátor,* the poet turned to the political situation of his times. *Az ember tragédiája* combines a look at history with a discussion of man's relationship to God. It is as if Madách had made a conscious effort to bring all these elements together in the last play he was able to complete.

Two months after finishing *Az ember tragédiája* Madách began to write *Mózes.* Eighteen months later he was ready to submit the drama for the Academy competition. Due to the time pressure, however, he could not avail himself of the benefit of Arany's advice on matters of poetic expression—advice which had proven so helpful in the previous work. The play retells in five acts the story of Moses from the time when the youth, educated as an Egyptian and serving as Pharaoh's adviser, meets the representatives of the Jewish people to the time of his death after having led the Israelites to the border of the Promised Land. Some of the highlights are the realization of young Moses that he is a Jew and his identification with the plight of his people; God's mission to him to lead the children of Israel to freedom; the anger of Moses, the Lawgiver, over the idolatry he encounters upon his return from the mountain; the decision to return to the desert from the border of Canaan so that the slave generation might die out and a new race, conscious of its freedom, might enter the land of milk and honey; and the final message of Moses to his people.

Perhaps this very listing shows what the judges of the contest saw as the play's main weakness and what the author himself seems to have been concerned about when he wrote to his friend Iván Nagy that he was aware of the fact that his work was different in form from the normal drama (ÖM 2, 931). The play is more epic than dramatic, and while it may be true that modern audiences are better prepared for the deviation from the traditional dramatic mode, as Dezső Keresztury claims, his attempt to depict this work as a forerunner of Bertolt Brecht's concept of the epic theater appears somewhat strained.[9]

In light of the fact that *Mózes* was written at a time when Madách was directly involved in the political affairs of his country as a parliamentary delegate, it is quite likely that the parallels between Hungarian conditions and those of his biblical account are not accidental. It has often been pointed out that the Jewish people could represent the Hungarians, trying to free themselves from the oppressive Austrian reign as represented symbolically in Pharaoh's Egypt. Aaron is frequently seen as Deák's counterpart, and Moses himself is interpreted as Kossuth or Széchenyi, depending on the critic's point of view. Madách certainly intended to do more than give a lecture on Hungary's past and present in the guise of a biblical drama, but his strong commitment to the ideals of Petőfi and Kossuth and his devotion to the laws of 1848, as evidenced by his political speeches, make it very probable that he was addressing his own nation when he had Moses exhort the Jews not to abandon the laws of the Ark of the Covenant.

György Lukács and others have occasionally attacked Madách's alienation from the people, and *Mózes* shows indeed—as does *Az ember tragédiája*—the great individual in conflict with the cowardly, uncomprehending, and hostile masses. What Moses tells Abiram seems to exemplify a callous contempt of the people, and the attitude of the towering historic figures whom Hegel saw as the movers of world history: "The people are just a silly tool / In the hands of some great individuals / Who write world history with their blood" (ÖM 1, 768). But as Sőtér rightly demonstrates, Madách's attitude was not this contempt for the people as such but a stand against what he saw as the large-scale demoralization of his compatriots which had its parallel in the faint-hearted views of the Israelites who longed for the fleshpots of Egypt and for their protected slave existence. Only liberty could bring an end to this demoralization.[10] And Moses comes to identify with the people whose leader God had appointed him to be. As he tells the Lord, "I have learned to live with the people and to die with them" (ÖM 1, 798).

Moses dies without entering the Promised Land. But a free nation will be established on the soil of the regained homeland. This optimistic ending is unambiguous and indicates the poet's new attitude. Although philosophically and artistically *Mózes* is anticlimactic after *Az ember tragédiája*, it constitutes a fitting conclusion of Madách's struggles.

Only fragments are left of the poet's last play. The first of the twelve scenes Madách had planned for *Tündérálom* was published in

Arany's literary weekly *Koszorú* (Wreath). The beginning of the second scene, a skeletal outline of the dramatic poem, and some notes for it were found in Madách's estate. There is enough to get an impression of the flavor of the work but not to speculate on the details of the plot.

After wrestling with profound questions of philosophy and in the wake of his active involvement in national politics, the poet seems to have felt a need to escape into the fairy world of Vörösmarty's *Csongor és Tünde*. The completed segment, which contains some of his best lyrical verse, reads like a whimsical parody of the opening scene of *Az ember tragédiája*, with Ilona the Fairy Queen resting on her throne, a choir of fairies singing, and the four fairies of song, charm (significantly named Tünde), whim, and imagination addressing their queen. Ilona is bored, and her thoughts go back to the wonderful times when humans could still sense and appreciate the magic of fairyland, when she found lovers in the sons of kings, in wandering knights and troubadours or shepherds whose hearts were filled with song. Today's technological world, in which ugly factories have replaced the castles and monasteries of old, has no room for those Romantic characters. When she is told that one such man is still left on earth, Ilona surmises that he must be a poet, hailing from Hungary, the land of the hero János, her last lover, the only country where even the "coal civilization" has not destroyed completely the dreams in the hearts of people who love their homeland. Ilona is going to seek out that dreamer. Amor appears, and his laments echo Ilona's longing for the past. Conditions have changed even on Mount Olympus; nobody takes him seriously now. And on earth true love has given way to commercialism; real estate registers and contract forms serve as shield and armor against his arrows; and he himself is being replaced by "newspaper advertisements, aunts, old hags, cosmetics, profiteers" (ÖM 1, 1062). The second scene has the Fairy Queen descend to earth, and then the manuscript ends abruptly in the middle of the young poet's monologue in which he reminisces about the great men of the past.

Madách's notes show that he had planned to bring various mythological figures—Hercules, Samson, Achilles, Helen—into his play and, perhaps more important, that he wanted to incorporate some motifs of traditional folktales, such as the prince with a pig's face whose spell is broken by a teardrop, and the lost fairy crown that changes into a girl. Having dealt in his dramas with Hungarian and world history, with biblical myth and philosophical speculation, the playwright appears to turn toward the popular culture that had inspired Petőfi and Arany. One of the two verse fragments the poet had jotted down for use in the conclusion of *Tündérálom* reads: "Your voices are new,/ I will return to you" (ÖM 2, 742). Madách's untimely death prevented his return.

CHAPTER 3

The Tragedy of Man: *Madách's Dramatic Masterpiece*

I   *From Eden to the Dusk of Mankind: A Synopsis of the Drama*

Az ember tragédiája is Madách's most ambitious literary project. He presents in fifteen dramatic scenes an overview of history from the creation to the final days of the human race.

The play opens with the Lord on his throne, surrounded by adoring angels. The noble task of the creation is completed, and God accepts the praise of the four Archangels and the angelic choir. Only Lucifer refuses to join. Instead, he sarcastically criticizes the work of the Creator who made man as an act of self-admiration. When Lucifer is threatened with eternal banishment, he defiantly demands his share of the world. "With scorn," he is granted two among the trees of Eden. But he is satisfied: this foothold of negation will suffice to bring down the divine order just established.

The second scene depicts Lucifer's pursuit of his destructive plan. Adam and Eve, enjoying a happy and sheltered existence in Eden, are to be his tools. He promises knowledge and eternal life if they disobey God's commandments. His appeal to their pride eventually succeeds: both eat of the forbidden Tree of Knowledge. Lucifer has won his first victory. But before Adam and Eve can savor the fruit of the Tree of Immortality, they are expelled from Paradise. Outside Eden they will try through hard work to build a new life.

The third scene shows this effort. For the first time, Lucifer's weakness is demonstrated in the encounter with the Spirit of the Earth who had earlier appeared in the choir praising the Lord. The force of negation can conjure up but not control the Earth Spirit. Adam now demands the promised knowledge. He wants to know the fate of those whose ancestor he is destined to become. Adam and Eve fall asleep, and the following eleven scenes are devoted to the dream visions of selected historical periods, created by Lucifer in order to demonstrate the futility of all human striving.

Adam's journey through time starts in ancient Egypt where he reigns supreme as a youthful Pharaoh, assisted by Lucifer, his minister. Slaves toil to erect a lasting monument to their ruler's glory. But upon Lucifer's probing, Adam admits that his power does not give him any joy. Suddenly a new world opens for him when a mistreated slave dies in front of his throne. Eve, appearing as the wife of the slave, irresistibly and inexplicably attracts Pharaoh. Through her, he senses for the first time the inhumanity of his system that makes millions labor for the benefit of one privileged individual. He grants freedom to all slaves. Yet he does not find rest. Lucifer, who shows him in a vision the transitoriness of all he had established, leads him on.

The scene shifts to Athens during the Persian Wars. Adam as Miltiades is fighting for his country, while Eve, as his faithful wife Lucia, is awaiting his return. Demagogues incite the people against the general, claiming that he has been bribed by the enemy. When the wounded hero arrives at the head of his army, the fearful mob professes allegiance. But Miltiades renounces his power by dismissing his troops, and the misguided crowd turns against him once more. Adam realizes that the people are not yet worthy of the freedom he had helped gain for them, and he asks Lucifer to show him a new world, one of enjoyment and sensuality.

This world of hedonistic pleasures is presented in the sixth scene. The drama's protagonist now appears as Sergiolus, a rich young Roman at the time of the Empire's greatest luxury and moral decay. In the company of friends, including Lucifer as Milo and Eve as a beautiful courtesan, he is enjoying an opulent feast while watching gladiator fights. But neither he nor Eve can find fulfillment in purely sensual experiences. As a funeral procession passes, Lucifer mockingly invites the dead body to join the frolicking group and prompts Hippia, another prostitute, to kiss the corpse. Without knowing it, she is exposing herself to the plague. Her agony is eased by Saint Peter who baptizes her. The apostle convinces Adam that there is a lofty goal worthy of his endeavor: Chrisitianity, the new doctrine of love and individual freedom, will rejuvenate a decaying society. A vision reveals the destruction of Roman civilization by barbarians while a fiery cross in the sky symbolizes the new era. Led on by Peter, Adam walks into a future that—as Lucifer knows—will hold more disappointments.

Constantinople during the Crusades is the scene of the next historical miniature. Adam, in the prime of manhood, is Tancred riding into
town at the head of his Christian knights. Lucifer is his shield bearer.
They are met with fear and distrust, as the citizens have had many
bad encounters with the Crusaders. The faith for which Adam had
fought is shown in its negative aspects: the theological dispute between Homoousians and Homoiousians becomes a bloody purge that
kills thousands; the Patriarch, entering the scene "in princely pomp
and state," preaches hatred of anyone whose views differ from his;
heretics are led to the stake; mendicant friars and sellers of indulgences complete the mosaic picture of what has become of the
"Church of Love." Adam rescues Isaura—Eve—from marauding Crusaders. Their love is doomed because she has been pledged to a convent. Adam cannot act against the demands of the Church. Ever
more clearly he recognizes the corruption of the noble doctrine that
has now turned oppressive and inhumane. He wearily asks Lucifer—
who has dallied with Isaura's maid in the meantime—to take him to a
more restful era.

But as Johannes Kepler, astronomer at the Imperial Court in
Prague, Adam cannot find inner peace either. He realizes the impossibility of living an isolated existence within society. Eve, as his capri-
cious and unfaithful wife Barbara, complains about the material dep-
rivations their marriage has imposed on her. With no comprehension
of his intellectual accomplishments, she presses him for more money,
forcing him to waste his time on worthless but profitable horoscopes
rather than pursuing his scientific interests. Lucifer, his famulus,
brings wine, and the famous astronomer tries to escape from his depressing reality into the dream of a better world.

The ninth scene—a dream within a dream—features Adam as Danton in the French Revolution. He exhorts the masses to fight for liberty, equality, and fraternity. But he senses that his own position is
threatened. When a young aristocrat and his sister—Eve—are brought
before him, he attempts to save them. In his conversation with Eve,
he recognizes the hopelessness of love in this period of terror. Only in
a world beyond—in which he cannot believe—would a final union
with her be possible. Despite his efforts, she is killed by one of the
sansculottes. But she reemerges, this time as a woman of the people
who has just committed murder in order to save Danton. She demands a night with the hero as her reward. Adam is horrified when he
discovers in her the features of the noble-minded young aristocrat. At
that moment Robespierre, Saint-Just, and other members of the Con-

vention approach to accuse Danton of various misdeeds. After predicting that Robespierre will soon share his fate, Adam bows his head beneath the guillotine. But before Lucifer can act as executioner, Adam awakens again as Kepler in Prague.

The tenth scene continues the action of the eighth. Kepler is pondering the significance of what he has seen. The lofty ideals of the French Revolution could not be completely obscured by the blood and terror he witnessed. Eve, in the meantime, has seen the shallowness and unworthiness of the courtier with whom she committed adultery. The scene concludes with a conversation between Adam and a student who has come to seek his advice on how to solve the mysteries of the universe. Adam points out that the most profound insight one can reach is the recognition of one's own limitations and basic ignorance. Science promotes prejudice, and the aspiring young scholar is encouraged to liberate himself from theory and tradition. Adam is led by Lucifer into a new era in which man's high ideals are rightly understood and thoughts may be freely expressed.

The subsequent London scene offers a vivid description of nineteenth-century capitalist society. Adam—now an elderly man— and Lucifer observe the colorful crowd milling about at a fair between the Tower and the Thames. There are merchants, workers, beggars, prostitutes, entertainers, and various representatives of the bourgeoisie. In the midst of the hectic activity Adam sees Eve— reincarnate as a middle-class girl—in the company of her mother. His offer to escort them through the crowd is sharply rejected because of his shabby appearance. When he follows Lucifer's advice and pretends to be a rich shipowner in disguise, he is welcome. Lucifer provides jewelry for Eve who is delighted that an execution will give her the opportunity to show off her gifts. But when she stops to place flowers at the statue of a saint, the jewels turn into snakes, and the money which Lucifer had given to a Gypsy woman serving as a go-between changes to mercury. Adam and Lucifer quickly withdraw. A *danse macabre* in which all figures of the scene join before leaping into an open grave is the conclusion. Eve alone, after dropping veil and cloak into the grave, ascends transfigured to the skies.

Adam and Lucifer move on to a utopian society of the future. A scientist in the Phalanstery explains to the visitors the strange relics of the past on display in the museum. He then tries to create artificial life in his laboratory, but the experiment fails as the Earth Spirit interferes. After the work period is over, punishment is meted out to those who have violated the community rules. Luther, Cassius, Plato, and Michelangelo appear as symbolic representatives of individualism that will not tolerate society's fetters. Finally, children who have reached the appropriate age are to be turned over to the communal education system. Eve, one of the mothers, tries to fight the separation from her child. Adam, rushing to her aid, is restrained by Lucifer. Once again, Adam and Eve realize that they love each other, a sentiment that seems totally anachronistic in this enlightened environment. Lucifer quickly leads him away.

The next scene shows Adam and Lucifer flying through space. The earth in the distance is growing smaller and smaller until it can hardly be distinguished from other stars. Lucifer tries to prompt his companion to break away completely from the earth's sphere of attraction. Disregarding the warning voice of the Spirit of the Earth, Adam continues his flight. Just as Lucifer believes he has won and triumphantly proclaims the victory of "the old lie," it becomes evident that man's ties to the earth are stronger. Adam will return for further struggle and further quest, and even Lucifer's sarcasm cannot shake his determination.

A desolate, frozen wasteland is the last station of their long journey. The sun has lost its warmth; the last humans are a few Eskimos, struggling to survive on a barren earth. Each neighbor is considered an enemy, threatening to decrease further the meager food supply. Consequently, an Eskimo, taking his visitors for unknown gods, implores them to assure that there will be fewer people and more seals. Adam recognizes in the coarse features of the Eskimo woman the face of Eve whom he has loved in so many reincarnations. Shattered by this encounter, he can only ask Lucifer to lead him back from the future into his present.

The final scene has Adam awakening in the spot where he fell asleep in the third scene. But Lucifer's visions of man's future have broken his spirit. A hint by his evil companion suffices to drive him to suicide. By ending his own life he can still prevent the dismal fate of all generations to come. Before he can carry out his decision, however, Eve comes to tell him that she is with child. Adam realizes that God has remained victorious, and he humbly bows before divine providence. Lucifer's furious outburst is silenced by the appearance of the Lord who is restoring His grace to man. Yet Adam's anxious questions about the future remain unanswered. Instead, the Lord urges him to trust and to face the struggle of life confidently with his wife at his side. Lucifer, too, will have a role in God's plan. He is to

serve as the leaven to keep man active. The poem ends with the repeated admonition to Adam to strive on and to trust.

II   *The Critics' Dilemma: The "Comedy of the Devil" or the Salvation of a Sinner?*

The comparative ease with which the plot of Madách's drama can
be summarized may be deceptive. At first glance, the poet's approach
seems straightforward. The historical visions are presented in chronological sequence. The first three scenes serve as exposition, the final
scene returns to the extrahuman sphere.

Yet even a cursory attempt to analyze Madách's message leads to
problems. Critics have been disagreeing on the poem's interpretation
for over a century. Books and articles have tackled the question of
whether it is essentially optimistic or pessimistic. The answers differ,
depending on the philosophical, religious, or political position of the
reviewer or on the *Zeitgeist* in general. Certainly no optimistic conclusion can be reached solely on the basis of the historical scenes. On
the other hand, the Lord's final words to Adam can only be understood as a promise to mankind. The differing interpretations, then,
spring mainly from placing the emphasis either on the frame, especially the last scene, or on the dream visions.[1]

Frequently, Lucifer as the creator of the visions of history has been
the center of attention. János Erdélyi, one of the earliest critics, took
Madách to task for his pessimism and for his attack on Fourier's socialist concepts in the Phalanstery scene.[2] He objected to a view of
history that stressed the gradual decline of the human race, and he
deplored the lack of balance in emphasizing man's relationship with
evil without showing the good in mankind. Lucifer, not Adam, seems
to be the main character. Thus, Madách should have called his play
"The Comedy of the Devil," not "The Tragedy of Man." [3]

Madách responded to Erdélyi's essay in a detailed letter. He obviously felt that Erdélyi should have dealt with the drama as it was
rather than suggesting what it might have been. In particular, he re-
sented the fact that his critic had paid no attention to the metaphysical setting and focused only on the historical visions:

What is meant to be the fundamental idea of my entire work is that once man
has broken away from God and is beginning to act, relying on his own

strength, the course of his action takes him, in succession, through the greatest and most sacred ideas of mankind to the very end. It is true that he fails everywhere and that what brings about his failure everywhere is a weakness that is hidden deep within human nature and that he cannot cast off (that, in my humble opinion, would be the tragic element). But, although he thinks in despair that all endeavors he has made so far have been a drain of energy, his development has gone ahead continuously, the human race has progressed although the struggling individual did not recognize it, and the guiding hand of God's providence makes up for that human weakness which he himself cannot conquer. This is what the "Strive and trust" of the last scene refers to. (ÖM 2, 876–77)

The particular scenes are arranged in such a way, Madách points out, that for the protagonist as an individual, each follows with "psychological necessity" from the preceding one. He concedes that he might have failed to clarify this sufficiently, but he rejects the accusation that he is mocking socialism. If that criticism were justified, he should also be accused of mocking liberty, Christianity, science, free trade, and all the other great ideas depicted. He sums up his objections to Erdélyi's misreading of his work by stating: "I would rather have written a bad *Tragedy of Man* in which I did not succeed in emphasizing great and sacred ideas than a good Comedy of the Devil in which I held them up to ridicule" (ÖM 2, 877).

Ágost Greguss, addressing the Kisfaludy Society in 1862,[4] saw the tragic element in "the disharmony of man . . . , who strives after the ultimate, but wishes to be independent of the ultimate; who longs to achieve infinite goals, but can envisage only finite ones; who, desiring freedom, becomes convinced of his bondage; who, over-confident of his spirituality, is prey to his materiality; who yearns for love, and reaps hatred; who desires knowledge and can achieve only enough of it to fathom his own ignorance; who thrusts himself away from his divine guide, and who ignorantly roams all over his unknown course."[5] But Greguss finds a positive resolution: the historical scenes do not show things as they are but only as Lucifer wants Adam to see them. While these scenes are not meant to be objective and accurate, they demonstrate "that for finite man, complete independence does not exist; he must depend either on God or on Lucifer, and he cannot tear himself away from the good without joining the forces of evil; he can overcome his disharmony and regain his lost peace of mind only if he once again submits himself in holy trust to God's providence." [6] For Greguss, the drama is a theodicy. He, too, sees mankind's progress through constant evolution. The prerequisite for this progress is that man never be satisfied in any one era.

János Arany also distinguished between Madách's views and those of Lucifer. In his 1862 speech in which he introduced the poet to the Kisfaludy Society, Arany asked: "Can we expect Lucifer to show Adam the future of mankind in other than pessimistic colors, since his goal is to drive Adam to despair, and to destroy in this way all his descendants in him? But it is said that the gloomy dream visions correspond to the facts of world history. This I deny. Despite all the accuracy with which the author presents the individual periods, it is apparent that Lucifer, in accordance with his objective, looks at the gloomier side. This is not the author's pessimism: it follows from the structure of the play itself" (ÖM 2, 1179). Thus, the drama is not pessimistic at all when seen in its totality.

Many critics have echoed the views of Greguss and Arany. Depending on their ideological position, they have either dismissed the historical visions as Lucifer's distortions or have attempted to show that Madách did not really depict all great ideas as having failed. The final admonition of the Lord is then interpreted as the encouragement to mankind to work for the creation of a better society.

Clearly, Lucifer's goal is the destruction of man. In order to break Adam's spirit, he has to present the future of the human race in the darkest colors possible while pretending to be showing reality. When he thinks he has succeeded, he openly admits his dishonesty: "So the old lie has triumphed!" (273). But eventually Lucifer fails. His plans have been frustrated by Eve's motherhood. And God's final promise seems to outweigh the message of Lucifer's visions. Arany's optimism appears justified.

Yet the reader is left with some uneasiness. Certain aspects remain unclear. If the historic visions are just Lucifer's distortions, why are in almost all scenes the seeds of something positive presented along with the negative features of the age? Saint Peter, for instance, provides a sharp contrast to the moral decay of the Roman Empire. On the other hand, the Lord does not invalidate what Lucifer has shown, and Adam's last words indicate his belief in the accuracy of the final vision: "But, ah, the end! If that I could forget!" (300). This "end" also corresponded to what Madách had found in some of his readings. Seen in this way, the poem is pessimistic after all, with God's concluding words but a compromise, lacking persuasive power and cred-

ibility. This, albeit without the implied rebuke, was the judgment of
Frigyes Riedl, and many critics have come to agree with him.

But in either case contradictions remain, and each side can produce evidence to support its position. The very problem Madách
raises leads to questions that go beyond the scope of a uniform drama
and that hardly permit unequivocal answers. What are the meaning
and the ultimate goal of the history of man who has broken away
from God and nevertheless remains under His protection and within
His plans? American scholar Thomas R. Mark correctly points out
that virtually all Madách criticism has been attempting to answer a
question that is never posed in discussions of other works of literature: "Is it true?" [7] But perhaps the author rather than his critics
should be blamed for that.

Madách used the term "tragedy." Is Adam truly a tragic character,
however, if the poem's exposition already assures Lucifer's defeat and
the salvation of man? The Lord's prediction in the opening scene is
quite succinct on this point when He tells the rebellious spirit that
the divine power will remain victorious (24). Is not the tragic figure
really Lucifer who is eventually denied what he could consider right-
fully his? The more accurate title, then, might be "The Tragedy of
the Devil."

But the protagonist of the play does experience a new tragedy in
each scene. Yet may we consider him an individual at all, is he capable of experiencing individual tragedy? He is the representative of all
mankind. And not Adam achieves victory but Eve, the embodiment
of womanhood whom God has given him as a companion.

In an attempt to salvage the unity of the drama, Mór Kármán
offered an interesting interpretation, later adopted by other scholars
as well.[8] Like Greguss, Kármán sees the poem as a theodicy. He focuses on the words of the Archangels in the opening scene. Gabriel
praises the Lord as "Idea," Michael hails him as "All-Might," and
Raphael calls him "All-Goodness" (20). According to Kármán, these
are key words since the entire drama takes place within God himself.
Adam represents divine power, Eve divine love, and Lucifer divine
wisdom. Above the three, divine unity is the all-embracing principle.
Jakob Overmans tried to show the absurdity of this view when he
asked what sense it would make for divine unity to forbid divine
power and divine love to eat the fruit of the two trees, or for divine
power to be kept in humble submissiveness through the knowledge of
its impending death.[9]

While Kármán's approach is no longer considered relevant, many modern critics also see a symbolic interpretation of the three principal figures as essential for the understanding of the work as a whole. István Sőtér believes that the play reflects Madách's era, a period that was aware of the forces of evil and yet had faith in progress. This progress arises from the interaction of the three "spheres" within the poem. The forces of nature, personified by Eve and by the Earth Spirit, struggle with the idealistic-moral forces associated with Adam, the embodiment of spirituality, and with Lucifer's sphere of doubt, negation, and materialism. Progress is possible when these three spheres are brought into harmony, which is achieved in the final scene.[10]

It may be helpful to deviate somewhat from the traditional approach to Madách's drama. If *Az ember tragédiája* is viewed as a monolithic entity, one cannot avoid the contradictions mentioned. But three different levels can be distinguished within the work. They are intertwined, to be sure, but separating them could make the author's message clearer. Only after each level has been examined individually does a look at the whole appear fruitful.

Az ember tragédiája is the tragedy of Adam, the individual. He confronts us in various historical incarnations, but behind each mask we observe the same man. In the conflict of ambitions and ability, ideal and reality, Adam is a Faustian individual. He is not an average person: his very nature and extraordinary character predestine him for the role of a tragic hero. In the company of the spirit of negativity, separated from God through original sin, he follows his path from one disappointment to the next up to his final desperation. The fact that he does not commit suicide does not alter his tragic fate: "Around me here all lives and smiles as gladly / As when I left. My heart alone is broken!" (289).

Adam's personal tragedy is to be distinguished from the historic visions that are the external cause of his repeated disappointments but also have a separate function within the drama. Through them, Madách probes the development of mankind. In rejecting some of Hegel's views, he arrives at a pessimistic position which, on the other hand, is quite realistic in the sense of the biblical message: there is no inner development of humanity, "for the imagination of man's heart is evil from youth" (Gen. 8: 21). Despite some apparent progress, mankind cannot achieve perfection after breaking away from God. Great ideas appear, but each carries the germ of future evil. The arrangement of the historical scenes shows how everything great and beautiful is desecrated and trampled on. In the end, there is not the triumph of science replacing a superfluous deity, nor the ideal human being capable of leading a moral life on his own. The final vision of man, regressing to an animalistic existence in complete isolation on a frozen planet, demonstrates that the supposed advancement was only a beautiful dream. This realization seals the tragedy of the individual at the same time. In its ultimate consequence, this view of history leads to nihilism: all values are not only reassessed but reduced to absurdity through the demonstration of their inevitable degeneration. Adam ends in despair; the world ends in nothingness.

But there is another level. Not only human forces interact in Madách's play, but extrahuman and supernatural powers are involved. The entire action—clearly tragic in itself—is placed in the framework of the traditional Christian mystery play, featuring the age-old contest between the principles of absolute good and absolute evil for the possession of man's soul. The Christian concept of an almighty God makes His victory a certainty. While Madách's Lucifer has little in common with the medieval devil, the confrontation remains the same. He is eternally inferior, rebelling against the Lord in senseless resistance. His plans are doomed before they can be brought to fruition. Thus the tragic fate of man is brought to a positive conclusion on this third level. What seems to end in hopelessness on earth is turned around completely in the divine sphere. In spite of all his errors and illusions, Adam is urged by the Lord to have confidence. This "in spite of all" is the final message. It is not a defiant rebellion but rather the result of a faith that demands constant struggle. The fact that the unmitigated gloom of the historic visions remains should prevent any shallow optimism.

An analysis of Madách's drama should note this structure. Because of it, critics have arrived at widely divergent positions and have accused the poet of hostility toward all religion and of paralyzing pessimism, or have found in his work only the confirmation of their own faith. Each time, only one level was considered and everything else appeared as mere decoration. A misreading of the whole was the inevitable result.

Due to the intertwining of the three levels, the play may lack perfect unity, and its final message may still be ambiguous. But Madách did not intend to leave us with a clear and programmatic statement. The concluding words of the play, "Hark to Me, Man! Strive on, strive on, and trust!" (300) do not provide a convenient answer to the questions raised but merely serve as a point of departure for individual reflections.

CHAPTER 4

Three Dramas in One: The Levels of Action in Madách's Tragedy

I Adam and Eve: The Tragedy of the Individual

SINCE Adam represents his entire race, it is not easy to see him as one individual with distinct features and a personal destiny. Furthermore, as he is not merely donning different historical costumes in the dream visions but truly becomes Danton or Miltiades or Kepler, there are inconsistencies in his portrayal.

Madách's selection of the introduction to the Book of Job is very skillful. By combining that symbolic account with the story of the fall of man from Genesis, he places the confrontation of the two extrahuman powers at the beginning of the world and of humanity whose representative is object and center of this contest. Adam's experiences are parabolic. He stands at the threshold of future history. His sin will be passed on to generations to come, as Lucifer tells him:

> Thy son shall suffer for thy deadly sins—
> Thy maladies thou wilt to him transmit.
> All thou hast mastered, all thou'st learned and felt,
> Shall be thy very own throughout the ages! (51)

Eve, too, is conscious of being the first link in a chain stretching into the distant future: "The only pride I know in this I find—/ That I shall be the Mother of Mankind!" (42).

Thus, Adam's decision to commit suicide goes beyond the intended destruction of his own being. Likewise, the Lord's eventual promise of renewed grace is meant for all mankind. Eve also points to this wider context in responding to Lucifer's taunt that her child, conceived in Eden, would bring only sin and sorrow to the world: "If God so wills, another Child of Sorrow / Will be conceived, who'll wash them both away / And fill this world of ours with Brotherhood!" (295).[1]

Madách thought he could combine all humanity in one character because he believed that man had remained essentially unchanged, that there had been no real inner development. His comment on his deeply pessimistic poem of 1857 "Szontágh Pál barátomhoz" (To My Friend Pál Szontágh) underscores this conviction: "I reread the poison with which I had filled Pál. Why did I not keep it to myself? So what? This poem is the truth, even if it is a tragedy, and human nature has never denied itself, and since Creation Adam has always appeared in constantly changing form, but he has always basically remained the same feeble worm, at the side of the even feebler Eve!" [2] This statement outlines the fundamental concept of his drama.

It is obvious from these remarks that Madách had conceived of his Adam as a prototype. He had determined the function of the play's protagonist in advance and then created scene after scene to support that function. Therefore, he could easily outline his basic ideas as he did in his response to Erdélyi. He deliberately appealed to the intellect rather than to the emotions of his audience and consciously wrote a philosophical poem. Of course, such orientation can interfere with a drama's artistic merits. This was the basis for Károly Zilahy's objection in the *Kritikai Lapok* as early as 1862 that has since been repeated by others: Madách was weak as a poet and even weaker as a playwright. *Az ember tragédiája* is a weak poem and an even weaker drama. It contains many beautiful ideas and philosophical thoughts, to be sure, yet the work is nothing but a "didactic poem in dialogue form." The principal flaw is that Adam is not individualized. "In each character, only Madách speaks; from the beginning to the end we hear only the witty voice of the author." [3]

Zilahy's criticism, while excessive, correctly identifies Madách's principal motivation in writing his tragedy. The fact that more than twenty years passed between the publication of the work and its first theatrical production indicates that Madách's contemporaries regarded it as a philosophical poem to be read, not as a true drama to be performed.

Given Adam's apparent role as the poet's spokesman, the question as to his individuality emerges even more forcefully. Is any character development possible in this case? Adam's external development is obvious. In his dream visions, he goes through the successive phases of an individual life-span. According to the stage directions, he is a "youthful" Pharaoh (53), "in the prime of life" as Tancred (114), reincarnate "as an Elderly Man" in London (194), "in the semblance of an aged man" in space (267), and a "broken-down old man" in the final vision (277). There is no specific reference to his age in the Prague and Paris scenes, but we can assume that he is of the same age as the historical figures he represents: Kepler was thirty when he succeeded Tycho Brahe as Rudolph's court astronomer, and Danton was executed at thirty-four. Thus these scenes are in their proper place with respect to Adam's aging process.

It is more difficult to trace a character development in him. But in rough outline we can witness in Adam the maturing process from impetuous youth to a thoughtful and introspective Kepler. In the London scene Adam demonstrates the desperate last love of an aging man, and later he becomes an increasingly passive and resigned observer. Some critics have interpreted this passivity as a philosophical or political statement, not as a result of aging.

In each of the visions Adam realizes that he has taken the wrong path. At the end of every scene he is heading in a new direction. What once was his ideal has turned out to be another chimera. Thus each scene lays the foundation for the next one. Throughout the play Adam essentially oscillates between two poles: life for himself or for others, egoism or altruism, individualism or collectivism. The historic episodes are also selected and arranged to reflect emphasis on the individual or on the collective body.

The young ruler of the fourth scene initially lives only for himself. He feels no bond to those whose destinies he controls. Therefore, he does not sense the bitter irony in Lucifer's words:

> Most honoured Master! Thy devoted servants,
> Who gladly would shed all their blood for thee,
> Seek anxiously to know why royal Pharaoh
> Sits brooding on his throne and cannot rest! (53)

Neither power nor sensual pleasures can satisfy him. He is motivated by the desire to become immortal through his accomplishments, but Lucifer soon demonstrates to him the dubiousness of such glory. Adam's egocentric shell is broken when the slave dies at his feet and when Eve appears. Only then can he hear the cries of anguish of his slaves, only then does he feel sympathy and can recognize the inhumanity of a system that makes millions work and die for one. He will devote his life to the service of those millions: the absolute king becomes an altruist turning toward the collective body, a people living in freedom and equality. Even his love for Eve cannot hold him back. Mankind has become more important for him than the ties to one individual.

As Miltiades, he embodies the noblest qualities of the community he had envisaged: honesty, dedication to the common cause, and willingness to sacrifice. But these very characteristics place him at odds with his environment, the same decaying Greek democracy that moved Plato to dream up his ideal state. Adam will be destroyed. But more significant than his downfall is his realization that he has pursued a phantom. He now recognizes how questionable the concept of freedom is in this degenerating world. So he turns to sensual pleasures and decides to remain indifferent to the concerns of others. Yet even as he places his head on the executioner's block he does not feel guilt since he has only served mankind's loftiest ideas.

As a young Roman, Adam appears shallow, egocentric, and self-indulgent. Human beings mean nothing to him. (His contempt now springs from his experience with his fellowmen in the preceding scene. As Pharaoh, he had no regard for others because of his ignorance of them.) He does not hesitate to pledge his lover Julia in a wager. The death of a man—particularly that of a slave—does not seem to touch him. But the superficial life fails to fulfill him; he realizes that something essential is missing. Once again Eve provides the first impetus and brings out in Adam what he had tried to suppress.

He happily embraces Christianity as the new idea which is worth fighting for. The collective body of which he wants to be part is a community of brothers. As a knight, he wants to protect and spread the new faith. Lucifer knows that another disappointment is in store for Adam. His sarcastic comment emphasizes the two divergent aspects of his companion's Faustian urge:

> What fires thee, Adam, is impossible,
> Though worthy, I admit, of Man's endeavour.
> It pleases God, because it points to Heaven.
> It suits the Devil, for thou'lt regret thy dream! (113)

Adam has indeed reason to "regret his dream": the Constantinople scene shows the degeneration of the pure faith proclaimed by Saint Peter. Instead of the expected ennoblement of man through religion, Adam witnesses the perversion of the "holy teachings" through human inadequacy. He had had a vision of a chivalrous Christianity of action, simple, meaningful, and fulfilling. So he cannot fathom the theological arguments: to him, not the divinity of Christ is at stake but people quarrel about an iota, and innocent human beings die as the result. Yet he does not regret his efforts on behalf of a cause that he still considers noble. But he is too disillusioned and too tired to undertake another attempt to change the world. He is longing for peace, for escape into the ivory tower.

Again he fails in the egocentric world he is trying to build for himself as Kepler. The conversation with Emperor Rudolph at the beginning of the scene makes clear that one cannot live in isolation but has to adapt to the society of which one is a part. In order to earn enough money for his superficial and pleasure-seeking wife, Kepler has to waste his time with astrological work which he despises. In addition, he is tormented by the realization that his knowledge is woefully inadequate. This period, too, does not correspond to the ideal conception he had had of it:

> I'd hoped to see an age when none would struggle,
> In which the daily round of social order,
> The sacrosanct conventions of the past,
> Would trouble no one, and at last I'd rest.
>
> . . . .
>
> That age had come. But what doth it avail me,
> If, in my breast, I feel the tortured soul
> That Heav'n hath handed down to foolish Man,
> The soul that may not rest and still must strive,
> And still would fight new fights . . . ? (160–61)

His restless urge takes him into an epoch that has the courage for change and renewal. Again, he wants to live for mankind.

"Liberty, Equality, Fraternity": Adam is now guided by the ideals of the French Revolution. He is filled with the desire to give to others the new order of things that he has recognized as correct. Everything individual—including his own personal life—is subordinate to the idea. Therefore, he may not pay attention to individual human beings. But this time, the reason is not Pharaoh's ignorance of others nor Sergiolus's contempt of men nor Kepler's escape into seclusion. In contrast to Tancred, he also knows that his efforts will not win him glory and that he will not fall in an open fight but rather as the victim of deceit and intrigue.

Through his talk with Eve, Adam becomes less sure of the rightness of his position. Again it is she who causes him to revaluate his views.

He displays respect for the courage to fight for ideas which he does not know or even opposes—a deadly weakness for a revolutionary! He recognizes the hopelessness that results from the abandonment of all religion. He also realizes, however, that it is too late for him to go in a different direction, guided by his individual conscience: "Conscience? The work-a-day world may enjoy / That privilege. But he whom Fate pursues / Has little time watching what's around him" (174).

The growing feeling of resignation in Adam is perhaps most strongly emphasized in this scene. He has tried once more to play a decisive role in shaping the fate of humanity, but he has failed again, due to the inadequacy of his environment and to his own faltering belief in his mission: for the sake of his love for Eve, he would have been willing to give up his philosophy. So he is not only calm as he places his head under the guillotine, but he seems relieved that a struggle that had lost its meaning will finally come to an end. This resignation explains why the Paris scene is the last one in which he carries the action.

The tenth scene represents a certain break in the drama's hitherto uniform structure. It constitutes the immediate continuation of the eighth scene. The action does not really progress at this point, and—contrary to the pattern of the preceding visions—the consequences of the previous experience are not shown. Yet this scene has an important function in clarifying the message of the poem. There is perhaps more philosophical discussion here than anywhere else in the play. It has been suggested that Madách created this second Prague scene (or rather divided the one scene into two parts) because of his concern about Austrian censorship. By presenting the potentially explosive topic of the French Revolution as merely a dream within a dream, its impact was blunted.[4] Different explanations have come from other scholars.

Anyway, this scene does not add to the characterization of Adam but mainly elaborates further on the theme of the limitation of human knowledge already broached in the eighth scene. Adam is yearning for a world where the individual can develop his potential to the fullest. He wants to embrace life in its totality and not just look at one aspect of it. But the dark features of this new society soon demonstrate how questionable the concept of freedom has become in the brutal atmosphere of early capitalism: "Is't independence if a thousand starve / Unless they will submit to one man's yoke?/ Why, that is but a dog-fight for a bone!" (232). In no other scene are all characters as much the products of their age as in this vision of nineteenth-century London.

The society Adam seeks now will no longer be ruled by extreme individualism and unlimited egoism but everybody will work for the welfare of the community. Science—no longer an end in itself as with Kepler but devoted to furthering the goals of the collective body—is to lead. Plato's ideas, combined with modern theories of social reform, will bring the longed-for fulfillment. Adam still has courage and believes in human progress, and hope is still the driving force in him. Paradoxically, this hope is Lucifer's gift to man, a thought typical of the age of negating *Weltschmerz* which found its philosophical expression in Schopenhauer: life was seen as negative—Lucifer also leads Adam and Eve to the Tree of Life—and consequently, hope, continuously trying to fill the senseless existence with meaning, is also a negative force.

The Phalanstery of the twelfth scene is the culmination of the concept of collectivity. But Adam is dismayed to realize that something essential is lost when individuality is no longer tolerated:

> No life, no individuality,
> That would allow a man to outdo his master!
>
> . . . .
>
> So Science, too, has disenchanted me.
> To me it seems a dull and childish school,
> And not the happy field I had expected. (249-50)

Again Eve serves as the catalyst. Through her, his doubts about the justification of this societal structure become a firm conviction: no community has the right to take away from the individual what is most personal and private to him. The relationship between individuals is what matters, not the organization of the collective body. He recognizes that particularly those things that escape rational interpretation are of the greatest significance for what is human.

The thirteenth scene in which Adam and Lucifer are flying through space represents another disruption of the drama's structure. Adam seems to have forgotten the ties to Eve, so important to him in the preceding scene. Eve does not appear at all. Adam is now trying to rid himself of all bonds. But the forces that pull him back to earth eventually prove stronger than his intensified individualism. Man rebels in frustrated pride against the Spirit of the Earth, but his rebellion cannot overcome the power that is even mightier than Lucifer himself.

The final decision is reached in this scene. Adam realizes that escape from the world is no solution. There will be struggle as long as man exists, but there will also be enthusiasm for ideals which does not lose its meaning if the ideals eventually turn out to be hollow. He now sees man's destination in the struggle itself, not in its desired outcome. Adam probably speaks for Madách:

> A hundred times my goal I'll vainly seek.
> It matters little. For what is that goal?
> 'Twill mark the end of a most glorious fight.
> The goal is Death, and Life is but a struggle.
> The struggle of itself is Man's real aim. (274)

This realization marks the moment when Lucifer has lost. It does not matter anymore how questionable the ideas are for which people fight. Adam has learned that the enthusiasm and willingness to work for an idea are more important than the idea itself.

This enthusiasm and willingness to work produce whatever progress there is in mankind. Now Lucifer, not yet ready to give up, has to show his aging companion the final stage of human history which is devoid of any idea. Man, sunk to the level of animals, is trying to prolong a meaningless existence by killing all his neighbors—a caricature of a world of unlimited individualism! It is only at this point that Adam demands to be led back to the present since he cannot bear this horrible future any longer.

The young man who awakens from his dreams is only in outward appearance still the Adam of the third scene. He has matured; his titanic pride has given way to gloomy resignation. He still sees suicide as a solution, but when he learns of Eve's pregnancy he realizes that this final attempt to reach a decision against God—which had actually been suggested by Lucifer and did not reflect his own free judgment—was doomed to fail: "Lord, Thou hast conquered! See, I'm in the dust!/ In vain I strove, without Thee, and against Thee!/ Raise me, or crush me, now . . . I bare my breast" (294). He humbly submits to the Lord's decision, but he will continue to be haunted by the vision of the depressing end.

The Book of Job had served as an inspiration to both Goethe for his *Faust* and Madách for *Az ember tragédiája*. But Madách's protagonist at the end of the play is much closer to his Old Testament model as he bows before God. He can find peace only in the forgiving grace of the Lord after having been driven ahead without respite—a precursor of rootless modern man—fleeing from the crowd or into the crowd, but always trying to escape from himself.

The inconsistencies in Eve's character are even more noticeable than those in Adam. At first glance, each scene appears to feature a different Eve, playing sometimes positive and sometimes negative roles. She is much more part of her environment than Adam. On the other hand, in Athens, as the young Marquise in Paris, and in the Phalanstery she provides a powerful contrast to her epoch.

When Eve is first introduced in the second and third scenes, she displays characteristics that Madách considered typically feminine. Her very first words show that she is more inclined toward enjoyment of life than Adam: "To live! To breathe! How sweet—how beautiful!" (26). Adam feels that he is destined to rule; she needs the feeling of dependence and of being cared for. Her ties to nature are closer than his; she is emotional and is not given to abstract reflections. She recognizes the meaning of the dance of the spirits of nature where Adam sees only "mummery" posing another riddle. When Lucifer refers to the two trees, her passionate reaction is immediate: "Ah, surely our Creator must be cruel!" while Adam remains skeptical: "But . . . if thou shouldst deceive me?" (34). A certain superficiality makes it easy for her to find an excuse for breaking the divine commandment. She places the responsibility on the Lord. She is less stable, can be tempted more easily, and tends to act without thinking. One of her striking traits is her vanity which gives Lucifer access to her and makes it possible for him to reach his further goal by promising her eternal youth and beauty. After their expulsion from Eden, she adjusts to the new situation by attempting to recreate the paradise they lost, albeit on a very modest scale. For the first time her maternal instinct becomes noticeable: she sees motherhood as her destiny. Beneath her changing historical costumes later on, this Eve remains recognizable throughout, with the various traits outlined here emphasized on different occasions.

Devotion to life characterizes her in the Egyptian scene. Her grief over the death of her husband is mixed with concern for her own existence and for her lost security. She finds a new task at Adam's side: the lonely Pharaoh is in need of devoted love that can draw him out of his egocentric world. Quite involuntarily she brings about a change in him. But she is incapable of following him, and she must not try to hold him back as he rushes forward into the future. After all

his roaming, he will return to her world of feeling. Thus, her words go
far beyond this particular scene and express her function for the entire poem: "Shouldst thou return, oh, King,/ With shatter'd hopes,
seek shelter on my breast" (71).

In Athens, Eve is Miltiades' worthy spouse. The contrast to her de-
generate surroundings is striking. Surprisingly, however, she seems
ready to believe the false accusations against her husband. Yet when
she sees Adam, she immediately realizes her grave error and stands by
him. But, again, she cannot find fulfillment at Adam's side: the Genius
of Death separates them.

In the Roman scene it is as if Eve had lost the strength to develop
her own personality. In her sensuality and superficiality she presents
a perfect mirror image of her times. She is seeking unconstrained enjoyment of life. And yet there is in her the longing for a higher and
meaningful existence. An almost unconscious memory of paradise
keeps her from finding satisfaction in the intoxication of the senses.
She is still aware of her task of providing an ennobling influence on
man: "Ah, what nobility, my Sergiolus,/ Thou couldst have found
here, in this soul of mine,/ Where thou hast sought for only passing
joy! (111). Ultimately, she becomes the cause of Adam's enthusiasm
for Christianity as his new goal. In his devotion to this new doctrine, a
changed attitude toward women emerges:

> Up! Up! And on to fight with might and main
> For the new faith, to fashion a new world
> Whose flower shall be expressed in knightly valour,
> While, in its poetry, on many an altar,
> Th'ideal Woman we shall see enshrined! (113)

But this "new world" assigns a different place to Eve. The Christian society of Constantinople has no room for individual happiness.
Eve's hopelessness comes through in everything she says, and again
she thereby moves Adam to seek another, a happier world.

In Prague, Eve once more seems to have been shaped by her surroundings. She is satisfied with conditions as they are, marked by old
prejudice but with enough leeway for her affirmation of life:

> I cannot bear the sight
> Of people with such sad and bitter minds
> That they must envy us this fair, bright world
> And dream they will replace it with another! (153)

She is completely incapable of grasping the intellectual heights to which Adam aspires. She does not recognize his inner nobility but rather deplores what she sees as her social decline as the result of her marriage. The science that he would like to pursue means nothing to her. Yet he is attracted to her, and she, despite her frivolous attitude, cannot bring herself to leave him either. Adam gives a fitting description of her character—and here, too, his remarks go beyond this specific episode. Behind her mask of superficiality he recognizes something transcending human frailty:

> How wondrously in woman do we find
> The base and noble mingled—gall and honey!
> Yet, why does she still charm us? It may be
> We know what is good in her is her own—
> The evil's of the age that gave her birth! (159)

Adam is aware of the conflicting nature of woman who is in part a mirror of her times and in part clashes with her age as an individual. Both characteristics are inseparably linked in her personality. In the Paris scene Madách exemplifies these aspects in two different female characters. The young Marquise faces Danton proudly and with her spirit unbroken. She awakens the conscience that he had suppressed so long. She stands by the old ideals and refuses to bow to the new powers. But she realizes the hopelessness of true human relations in the atmosphere of the Revolution, and the only possibility she sees for a reunion with Adam is in a world beyond the grave. The individual is crushed by the environment: there is as little hope for Danton and the Marquise as there was for Tancred and Isaura. But another Eve appears in this scene, carnal and unfettered by convention. She has killed in order to save Adam and is now claiming her just reward. Horrified, he recognizes in her, too, the features of the woman he loves:

> The self-same face, and form, and mode of speech—
> And yet, in ev'ry way, some little thing
> That cannot be described, I miss in her,
> And so she has become another being!
> She whom I sought was shielded by a halo—
> This one repels me, for she reeks of Hell! (179)

Both women together reveal the true face of his era that he had been unable to see because his ideals had clouded his vision. But he also

understands that the two different Eves are only the two extreme aspects of one mysterious being: Woman Eternal:

> Were those two women also only dreams?
> Or, should I say, one woman with two shapes,
> That come and go, as destiny may will,
> Like surging waves, that change from bright to dark! (184)

In the *danse macabre* at the end of the London scene Eve drops her
veil and cloak into the open grave and ascends, transfigured, to the
skies—a symbolic representation of Woman Eternal emerging after
the negative aspects of the times have been stripped off.

In the utopian community Eve once more plays a significant role.
She is all mother in this scene, struggling desperately against a society
that is bent on breaking the most natural ties between human beings.
Like an apparition from times past, she fights for the rights of the
individual, for the right of a mother to her child, for the right of
choosing one's partner freely. When she is told that the restoration of
the family unit would threaten "the fruits of holy Science," she exclaims: "What does this chilly Science mean to me?/ If Nature wills
it, let them be destroyed!" (263). Through her, Adam sees how much
the collective state of his dreams violates human nature.

The space scene has no room for woman with her close ties to nature. Human relations do not matter to Adam at this point. Eve appears again in the oppressive vision of the icy wasteland. Just as nature is dying, so Eve has sunk to the lowest level. Lucifer hopes to
break Adam completely by showing him how woman has become an
animal. Adam tries in vain to escape from this sight:

> I will not look! Though Man has sunk so low
> That he now seems disgusting to our eyes,
> The sight of him does but awake contempt.
> But if Woman, th'ideal, human poem,
> Hath also turned into a travesty,
> She'll make us shudder! . . . Come, I will not see her! (286)

He will never forget this nightmarish image in which nothing is left of
the female ideal that had inspired him so often.

In his journey through history Adam has encountered a constantly
changing Eve, but fundamentally she has remained the same. She
represents the extreme spirit of each age envisaged by Adam and thus

forces him to reconsider his idealistic fantasies. She serves as a catalyst and spurs him on to renewed searching; she points to new ideals. But from her first appearance in Eden she has continued to embody the two functions that Madách associates with womanhood: she ennobles, stimulates, and inspires—but she also drags man down. "Gall and honey" are her characteristics.

Adam needs Eve as a complement, and he also needs her as an echo for his own personality. Even before their paradisal peace in Eden is disturbed, he tells Eve:

> What is a sound when there's none to perceive it?
> What is a ray not caught up by some colour?
> What were I, if, unechoed, unreflected,
> My being could not find another being,
> Whereby to get enamoured of myself? (29)

But Eve is not merely that passive echo. In the *danse macabre* of the London scene she names the three concepts whose embodiment she is: "I'll shine beyond the tomb!/ While Love and Poetry and Youth endure,/ Upon my homeward way I still will go" (236). Fifteen-year-old Etelka Lónyay had inspired young Madách to write his first lyric poetry. This inspiration is now seen as a universal force. Therefore, the references to "poetry" in connection with womanhood in the Phalanstery scene and in the ice region are not accidental. The words of the Lord at the end of the play underscore the function and responsibility of woman. He promises Adam that there will always be a divine voice providing guidance:

> Obey that voice! And should its heav'nly tones
> At times be deadened by the stress of life,
> The purer spirit of this tender woman,
> Less stained than thou art by the love of self,
> Will surely hear it. Through her heart 'twill flow,
> And turn, in thine, to Poesy and Song!
> With these two aids, beside thee thou wilt find,
> In good or evil fortune, constantly,
> The consolation and the smile of Genius! (299)

These lines demonstrate how much the author's attitude toward women had changed since the time when he had referred to the "even feebler Eve" who accompanied the "feeble worm" Adam.

Eve stands as the driving and uplifting force at the side of Adam whose intellect will never be able to arrive at the ultimate solution. She represents an element of vitality through her motherhood. This is a force that renders Lucifer powerless. To him, motherhood is only the perpetuation of human suffering. But the affirmation of life wins out against the force of negativism.

In his poem about Cain's slaying of Abel, "Az első halott" (The First Death), Madách concludes with a stanza that describes Eve's role as well:

> It was the icy intellect and searching bosom of the male
> That placed man into his grave;
> The feeling heart and trusting voice of woman
> Lifted our soul to its eternal home. (ÖM 2, 142)

While Eve's function in the drama and her impact on Adam emerge very distinctly, Madách is not consistent in outlining the relationship between dream visions and reality in her case. Lucifer promises to show the future to both Adam and Eve. Yet—in contrast to Adam—Eve does not age during the dream sequence. She does not recall past visions in any of the historical scenes. Upon awakening, she gives no evidence of having gone through the same devastating experiences as her husband. Only Adam appears to have dreamed; Eve is but a part of his dream visions. She therefore always represents the age that Adam has entered, and she is always shown from his vantage point. Károly Szász was the first to observe that both Adam and Eve fall asleep but that only Adam is dreaming.[5] This may seem a minor point, but it correctly stresses the one-sidedness of Adam's perspective.

The attempt to identify the author with the persona of a literary work is a dubious undertaking at best. Yet it is obvious that some events in Madách's life had an impact on certain aspects of the tragedy of Adam and Eve. This does not mean, however, that the entire play should be regarded as an autobiography in disguise as has been claimed on occasion.

Many of Madách's personal experiences were directly connected with his public life and with conditions in his country. The spectacle of demagoguery and political corruption that Adam witnesses in Athens may have been inspired by Madách's involvement in county politics. It may also reflect, as Marcell Benedek suggests, the author's reaction to "the first free parliamentary election in 1848, during which an inflamed mob rejected the most genuine and zealous friend

of the people, Sándor Petőfi, and pelted him with stones" (13).
Benedek's interpretation of Pharaoh's freeing of his slaves as an expression of Madách's satisfaction with the decision of the Hungarian
nobility to abolish serfdom is debatable. But the attempt of Adam as
Kepler to retreat into the seclusion of his study corresponds closely to
Madách's attitude after his divorce from Erzsi. Significantly, however, the second Prague scene concludes with Adam's resolution to
break out of his self-imposed isolation. It is likely that Madách re-
called his legal experience at Balassagyarmat when he had Adam say
in the London scene:

> I bless my fate! I was not made a judge.
> When one is lounging in a snug arm-chair,
> 'Tis easy to lay down the law to others,
> So easy to pass sentence casually . . .
> But hard for him who probes hearts to their depths! (229)

Most scholars agree that the failure of Madách's marriage had a
strong impact on his dramatic poem, particularly on his portrayal of
Eve. His poetry from the time after his divorce offers parallels to the
male-female relationship as shown in his drama. So he writes in "Egy
vetélytárshoz" (To a Rival):

> Surely, woman's mind and her desire are fickle!
> A dreary wasteland is the realm of her heart,
> And if there is the trembling brilliant magic above her,
> Inspiring song and salvation, it does not radiate from her,
> But it is our soul which throws a flood of light upon her.
> What did I lose after all? Idols tumbled down
> In my heart—it means nothing that, with them,
> I threw out the god in my soul;
> And I am sitting alone in my desolate world.
> The devil comes and comforts me with scorn:
> "Be happy! You lost an unfaithful wife, a false friend,
> There is nobody to diminish your share,
> You are the master over the whole world." (ÖM 2, 357)

It is the author of *Az ember tragédiája* whose bitterness comes to the
surface in these lines.

It would be wrong to trace the pessimism of the historic visions
exclusively to the disappointments of his private life. But there can be
no doubt that Eve, especially in the role of Barbara Kepler, is pat-

terned after Madách's unstable and unfaithful wife. Almost all of her
utterances reflect Madách's marital experience, from her reference to
her husband as the "poor dear man" who "is ill, . . . ah, very ill"
(153) and her request, "Johannes. I need money very badly" (155) to
her adulterous behavior which—as in Erzsi's case—results from her
shallowness and frivolity, not from any deep-rooted passion. While
Az ember tragédiája is certainly more than a poetic expression of private concerns, it does show the inner development of the poet who is
overcoming his disillusionment and depression and does not become
an unremitting •misogynist like Strindberg. (But it is interesting to
note that Madách dealt with Strindberg's recurrent theme of man
suffering at the hand of woman at a time when it had not yet become
commonplace in literature.) Madách recognizes the more profound
and ennobling aspect of "Woman Eternal." Surely his first deep love
had left a mark and also affected his portrayal of Eve, but Voinovich's
suggestion—echoed by others—that the Marquise in the Paris scene is
a poetic memorial to Etelka is questionable.

Eve's motherhood brings about the solution of man's tragedy. This
points to the woman who probably exerted more influence on the
poet than anybody else: his strong-minded mother. It was she and not
his own wife who served as the model for Eve as a mother in the
Athens and Phalanstery scenes. Madách's strong ties to his mother
and his gradual coping with the failure of his marriage led to a new
attitude toward woman which, in the final analysis, also determined
the function of Eve in his play.[6]

II   *The Future as a Bad Dream: Madách, History, and Hegel*

In his attempt to demonstrate to Adam the futility of all human
endeavor, Lucifer places him in constantly changing historical con-
texts in order to show that man will always fail in his undertakings.
He intends to prove through this one-sided view of history that there
is only meaningless circular motion instead of development and perfection. But Adam continues to see some progress in the course of
history until the last of his dream visions shatters his illusions.

History is thus much more than decorative background in
Madách's drama. It rather serves as the foundation of the principal
part of the play. By presenting different significant periods from the
annals of mankind—and through their structurally determined
sequence—the poet was able to make Adam the embodiment of various ideas that have been important in the development of humanity.

In this way he could also show the continuous repetition of the tragedy of the Faustian individual who has at all times clashed with the masses. Only the realm of history gives Adam the opportunity to develop all his potential positive and negative qualities.

Madách felt free to use historical facts as he saw fit. He was more concerned with illustrating the spirit of a particular period than with objective scholarly presentation. Thus, certain anachronisms are quite intentional, as are deviations from geographical or historical reality. Because of his intention to emphasize the *Zeitgeist* of each epoch, he had to allot much space to the depiction of background. The clearer the surroundings are sketched out, the clearer Adam emerges as an historical personage. A close look shows how economical Madách is in his portrayal. Each secondary character contributes to the task of bringing to life the particular age, each statement has a specific function, and there is only a minimum of unnecessary embellishment. An investigation of the specific sources for the historic details is not particularly enlightening. Edward Gibbon's monumental work on the decline of Rome, Edmund Burke's study of the French Revolution, Johann Ludwig Christian Breitschwert's Kepler biography, the volumes on world history by J. B. Schütz and Karl von Rotteck, and many other books merely furnished the raw material that Madách utilized according to his needs.

The nine historical periods appear to be carefully selected and arranged.[7] It is hinted, to be sure, that Adam went through additional epochs. He mentions his participation in the battle of Philippi and is reminded of the fact that he once held Semiramis in his arms. There are references to his fight for the cause of liberty at Chaeronea and to his support of Emperor Constantine, and he remembers Aspasia's embraces. But Madách realized that additional scenes would not have further clarified his intended message. So these allusions merely serve as a reminder that Adam has indeed gone through all of man's history.

For Madách, history is not an accidental accumulation of isolated facts nor a mechanical process in which the individual plays but a limited role. It is rather the spiritual sphere in which the question about the meaning of life and of human activity is posed most clearly. An equally clear answer, however, is difficult to find. It is Lucifer, after all, who produces and interprets the historic visions in the spirit of absolute negativity. His one-sidedness is somewhat balanced by Adam's positive views. Yet even God's final statement does not deny the validity of Lucifer's visions, and much of what is shown to Adam represents Madách's own conclusions. In the final analysis, only faith can answer the question whether history is a meaningless repetition of human folly or a demonstration of divine providence.

The quest for meaning in the flow of human history has occupied historians and theologians for centuries. Given Madách's interest in both history and philosophy, it can be assumed that he was familiar with the interpretation of mankind's development by one of the leading philosophers of his century. The first edition of Friedrich Hegel's *Philosophy of History* was published in 1837. Three years later the philosopher's son brought out an expanded edition of Hegel's lectures. The third edition appeared in 1848. Each could have come to Madách's attention, even though Hegel is not listed among the authors represented in his library. But striking parallels in general concepts and in details and the dialectical arrangement of the historical scenes in *Az ember tragédiája* suggest the poet's acquaintance with his work.

In his approach to history Hegel is an heir to the philosophy of Enlightenment. To him, what is real is rational, and what is rational is real. When looking at history, we are observing matters spiritual rather than material: "The phenomenon we investigate—Universal History—belongs to the realm of the *Spirit*." [8] The substance and the essence of the Spirit is freedom, and the history of the world is the progress of the consciousness of freedom. This progress, the development of mankind, generally takes place in three steps. Here Hegel applies the dialectic principle: an idea or situation—the thesis—already potentially contains its opposite—the antithesis—which it develops and against which it struggles. Eventually, the two opposites are united on a higher level—the synthesis. All history can thus be divided into three major periods:

The Orientals have not attained the knowledge that Spirit—Man *as such*—is free; and because they do not know this, they are not free. They only know that *one is free*. But on this very account, the freedom of that one is only caprice. . . . That *one* is therefore only a Despot; not a *free man*. The consciousness of Freedom first arose among the Greeks, and therefore they were free; but they, and the Romans likewise, knew only that *some* are free—not man as such. . . . The Greeks, therefore, had slaves . . . which made that liberty . . . only an accidental, transient and limited growth. . . . The German nations, under the influence of Christianity, were the first to attain the consciousness that man, as man, is free: that it is the *freedom* of Spirit which constitutes its essence.[9]

Man—as "subjective spirit"—has an innate "impulse of *perfectibility.*" [10] This impulse pushes the development of mankind forward to the creation of the state. Therefore, history in the real sense of the word exists only where there are states.

The World Spirit, the universal reason, uses as the agents for its realization within the state and for the state what Hegel calls "World-Historical Individuals." [11] Their effort and their passion bring about progress, since nothing great can be accomplished without passion. They resist the traditional course of things and take their justification not from existing conditions but from the Spirit to be realized which is still hidden from the masses. The fate of such a hero is frequently unhappy. He stands alone and is misunderstood, people attack his passion as a moral shortcoming and often succeed in bringing him down—after his historic mission has been fulfilled. The "World-Historic Individual" has only one purpose in life and cannot be impeded by his environment: "So mighty a form must trample down many an innocent flower—crush to pieces many an object in its path." [12]

Hegel combines his concept of historic progress with another idea that can be traced back to antiquity. Like Roman historian Florus, like Saint Augustine in his *City of God*, or like Herder, he, too, establishes an analogy between the periods of world history and the aging process of the individual. Because of the significant differences between the cultures of Greece and Rome, he divides the world of classical antiquity—the antithesis to the Oriental world—into two periods. There are, then, four steps in the development with four corresponding political systems: Despotism (the Orient), Democracy (Greece), Aristocracy (Rome), and Monarchy (the Christian world). The ideal monarchy in which each citizen participates in the perfection of the state ranks highest in his view.

The Oriental culture is humanity's infancy. Spirit and nature are not yet divided. One despot rules; everybody is subject to his will. The second step is the separation, the reflection of the Spirit in itself. This step takes place in two phases: in Greece, the adolescence of mankind, the Spirit has achieved a certain freedom but is still bound to matter; in the Roman state, the manhood of history, the free individuals are sacrificed to the severe demands of the national objects. The next stage is that of the Germanic culture. If the analogy to the development of a human being were upheld, this Christian world would have to represent mankind's old age. But Hegel—like Florus

before him—is hesitant to depict his own period as humanity's senes-
cence. Natural old age means retrospection and physical and mental
weakening, but the Christian epoch of the Spirit is the stage of perfect maturity, the return to unity. The Divine Spirit has entered the
world and has established itself in the individual who only now can be
completely free. Therefore, the analogy breaks down at this point.

This chronological sequence corresponds to a geographic progression. History follows the course of the sun: "The History of the World
travels from East to West, for Europe is absolutely the end of History,
Asia the beginning . . . Here rises the outward physical Sun, and in
the West it sinks down: here consentaneously rises the Sun of self-
consciousness, which diffuses a nobler brilliance." [13] In Europe,
Christianity—which had originated in the East—encounters the
young Germanic peoples. This fusion of the East and the West is of
major significance and marks the beginning of the last historic age.

Within the Christian world there are again three dialectically related epochs. The first stretches from the emergence of Germanic
tribes in the Roman Empire to the reign of Charlemagne. The second
one is characterized by the externalization of the original inner principle of Christianity: Christian freedom becomes bondage. But this
transitional period is necessary for the realization of the Spirit. The
third stage begins with the Reformation and includes the philosopher's own era. Freedom is restored in a more profound manifesta-
tion. Reason becomes the new guide, not custom and tradition as before. All rights have to be legitimized as being based on reason. In this
respect, the French Revolution, the last event Hegel deals with in his
lectures, is closely related to the Reformation and stands as a necessary world-historical phenomenon.

Hegel claims that those three stages of the Christian age could be
considered as the periods of the Father, the Son, and the Spirit. The
realm of the Spirit is the harmonizing of the antithesis. The study of
history merges here with theology. In the introduction to his work
Hegel had referred to Leibniz and his *Theodicy*. At the end of his
book Hegel feels that he has made his point: "That the History of the
World, with all the changing scenes which its annals present, is this
process of development and the realization of the Spirit—this is the
true *Theodicæa*, the justification of God in History. Only *this* insight
can reconcile Spirit with the History of the World—viz., that what
has happened, and is happening every day, is not only not 'without
God,' but is essentially His Work." [14]

In Madách's tragedy the visions of history are produced by Lucifer in order to lead man away from God. Thus, as in Hegel, the contemplation of human history is embedded in a metaphysical framework. But, given Lucifer's intentions, his depiction of history is meant to lead to different conclusions. Madách's selection of historical scenes and many of their details suggest Hegel parallels. He goes beyond Hegel in the time frame of his visions, to be sure; he even depicts future stages in the development of mankind. But he, too, emphasizes the French Revolution. Adam is seen here for the last time as actively determining human history. In the London scene, in the Phalanstery, and in the ice region, he is a mere observer, approaching history from the outside and no longer attempting to influence the course of events. In the Eskimo scene history in Hegel's sense has ceased to exist—there is no longer any trace of the structure and order of the state. The period of Adam's active involvement in the roles of various "World-Historical Individuals" thus parallels exactly the period covered by Hegel.

In the selection and arrangement of his historic scenes Madách follows closely the scheme established by Hegel. Egypt—treated by Hegel in detail as an example of the Oriental stage—is succeeded by the Hellenic period as an internally necessary further development. The Roman Empire follows, and within that stage, Christianity emerges as the new determining factor in world history. The connection with the Germanic nations is emphasized in the vision of the "half savage hordes" of "shaggy and barbarian warriors" at the end of the Roman scene (111–12). Tancred is the representative of the new Christian epoch. A new social structure develops under Christianity, marked by the opposing powers of church and state. This conflict is characteristic of the second Christian phase which features, according to Hegel, the consistent development of two rival forces into theocracy and feudal monarchy. Madách's Prague scene, essentially pre-Lutheran in spirit, reflects this stage. The final epoch—which brings about true spiritual freedom—begins with the Reformation. In the Catholic world the French Revolution is to play a role similar to that of the Reformation for Protestantism. Danton functions here as Madách's "World-Historical Individual," fighting for human liberty and a world based on reason.

Madách, too, emphasizes the course of history from the Orient to the Occident. In the ice region Adam seems to quote Hegel:

> Oh, take me to my land of swaying palms,
> That lovely land of sunlight and sweet scents

> Where surely now the soul of Man has grown
> And blossomed into full self-consciousness! (278)

The panorama of history in *Az ember tragédiája* starts in the East, in Egypt, and moves to the West, to Greece and Rome. As in Hegel, the emergence of Christianity in the Roman world provides the major turning point. The transition to the Germanic realm in the North occurs here: Tancred appears as the representative of the North. And the new religion inaugurates an era whose "Sun of self-consciousness" also rises in the Orient. Therefore, Madách's scenes depicting the Christian culture again go from the East (Constantinople) to Prague and further West to Paris and London.

The parallel between the growth of an individual and the stages of history is quite obvious in Adam's aging process. As a young man, he represents the young world of the Orient and of antiquity. With Christianity, he reaches in Tancred "the prime of manhood." Then there is a certain deviation from Hegel's scheme: with the London scene—Madách's own period—old age sets in. In the Phalanstery Adam wants to enjoy what past efforts have accomplished: "Then lead me on and let my soul delight / To share the happiness which oft Mankind / Had fought and strained for and deserv'd to win!" (239). In the space scene and even more in the ice region Adam is an old man. With the cooling of the sun, the earth and human history have come to an end.

For Madách, world history also appears as the "progress in the consciousness of Freedom." In Egypt Adam as Pharaoh is the "one" considered "free." Everybody else is subject to his will: "Why does a slave exist? To carry stones / To the King's pyramids, and die as soon / As he's disabled. Millions die for one!" (59). But Adam is not a free man himself, he is the prototype of Hegel's "despot." Since Madách selected mainly periods of transition for his historical visions, the change to the Hellenic world is already indicated in this scene. Adam renounces arbitrariness and despotism because he—and thus mankind—is becoming conscious of freedom. By liberating his slaves, he is freeing himself.

But in classical Greece and Rome, the concept of freedom is not yet shared by all. Even though there is no longer a one-man rule, there are still slaves, and Madách touches upon this discrepancy on several occasions. The same basic quality takes different forms in free men and in those in bondage. Eve, as a noble Athenian woman, points out:

> A mighty voice inspires our souls—
> Ambition. In the slave, indeed, 'tis hush'd.
> Or, if 'tis heard, is cramp'd by dreams of crime.
> But Freedom, warming it with its own blood,
> Makes it as glorious as a civic virtue.
> So it engenders all that's rare and great. (73–74)

The external termination of slavery does not produce any change as long as social circumstances do not allow the freed man to realize his freedom. Thus, Crispos, whom Miltiades had redeemed from slavery, is among those who demand the general's death. As Eve reproaches him, he retorts: "Forgive me, lady. Only he or I / Can hope to live. Alas, I have three children,/ And he who bids me yell supports us all!" (80). The young Roman Catulus expresses most brutally the condition of those still deprived of their freedom: "*Recipe ferrum* . . . Coward! . . . I have slaves / Enough without thee, and I am not greedy" (98).

Christianity brings about a fundamental change. Hegel had stated that under Christianity slavery is impossible, since man is man, is contemplated in God, and God will have all men to be saved. Greek freedom was accidental and still conditioned by slaves and oracles; but now the principle of absolute freedom in God emerges.[15] This view is echoed in the words of Saint Peter:

> Then let thine aim be to exalt the Lord,
> In all thy work! Yet ev'ry man is free
> To make the most of what is best in him,
> If he but does what is ordain'd by—Love. (113)

It does not matter that his new world of "Brotherhood and Individual Freedom" (112) does not materialize as the ideal society. The higher stage of development achieved through Christianity is more significant in the spiritual realm than in the sphere of matter. Actually, Hegel and Madách describe in very similar terms the negative aspects of the period governed by the Church. Christianity, however, is the first truly universal movement, and Adam embarks on the new course not as a Roman citizen but as a citizen of the new world to be created.

Adam represents Hegel's "World-Historical Individuals." As a fictitious Pharaoh, he takes the step to the freedom of the Hellenistic world. As Miltiades, he is one of those heroes who fall after accomplishing their historic mission. As Sergiolus, he seems a mere reflection of Roman society, but by embracing Christianity—whose significance he is the only one in his surroundings to recognize—he makes a "world-historic" decision. Tancred is another of those towering loners, as is Kepler who is far ahead of his age. The last of these movers of history is Danton. It is no accident that Adam is nameless in the remaining scenes.

Especially as a young man, Adam pursues his goals with the passion that Hegel saw as typical of his heroes. But even the aging Adam castigates the "dull sobriety" of the utopian society which punishes great men like Luther, Cassius, Plato, and Michelangelo for their passionate nonconformity. Like Hegel's prototype, Adam has a single motivation in each scene. He cannot be concerned about obstacles. When Lucifer asks Tancred what he would do, were the mob to question his right to lead, the response is, "Where the right spirit burns will victory be . . . / And I could crush the mob" (116).

Adam does not find personal happiness in his accomplishments. Miltiades and Danton are among those who are toppled after fulfilling their "world-historic" mission. What brings them down is mainly, as Hegel phrases it, "envy—vexed at what is great and transcendant—striving, therefore, to depreciate it, and to find some flaw in it." [16] This attitude is particularly obvious in the Athens scene. When Eve demands to know of whom the bloodthirsty mob is raving, she is told: "Of one who overtops his fellow-men,/ And who, for that alone, offends them all" (80). Miltiades recognizes the uselessness of defending himself before those who moments ago had paid tribute to him: "The People never would forgive its shame!" (91).

Besides Crispos, the only person in the Athenian mob to be singled out by an individual name is Thersites. Hegel had referred in the same context to "the Thersites of Homer who abuses the kings" as being "a standing figure for all times." [17] Of course, one can find some human weakness in any great person. Hegel's "well-known proverb," quoted in the same connection, that "no man is a hero to his *valet-de-chambre*," is echoed by Lucifer in the London scene: "And no one sets much store upon the present,/ Nor does a man seem great in his own bedroom" (222).[18]

While details in the Egyptian, Greek, and Roman scenes could have been inspired by Hegel—from the motivation of the pyramid builders to his condemnation of the Athenian demagogues and of the Roman decadence that considered murder an adequate public entertainment—the parallels are particularly striking in the description of the age of the Crusades. Hegel sharply criticized the bloody excesses of those who professed to serve God. This was the period when the Church reached the completion of its authority. The terror of the Crusades led directly to the Inquisition of later centuries. For Madách, the fire that burns heretics is the symbol connecting Constantinople and Prague.

The Constantinople scene in *Az ember tragédiája* dramatically highlights Hegel's description of that city and period:

At Byzantium Christianity had fallen into the hands of the dregs of the population—the lawless mob. Popular licence on the one side and courtly baseness on the other side, take refuge under the sanction of religion, and degrade the latter to a disgusting object. In regard to religion, two interests obtained prominence: first, the settlement of doctrine; and secondly, the appointment to ecclesiastical offices. . . . Violent civil wars arose, and everywhere might be witnessed scenes of murder, conflagration and pillage, perpetrated in the cause of Christian dogmas. . . . In the contest on the question whether Christ were ὁμοούδιοδ or ὁμοιούδιοδ—that is of *the same* or *similar* nature with God—the one letter ι cost many thousands their lives. . . . The Idea of Spirit contained in this doctrine was thus treated in an utterly unspiritual manner. The appointment to the Patriarchate at Constantinople . . . and the jealousy and ambition of the Patriarchs likewise occasioned many intestine struggles.[19]

This is the atmosphere that Tancred encounters and to which his naive idealism provides an effective contrast. The sale of indulgences he witnesses was also among the symptoms of the corruption of the true faith condemned by Hegel.

The Prague scene further illustrates this corruption. Hegel had stated that among Catholics, heretics as well as witches were persecuted, that one might even say they were placed in one category.[20] Madách's scene starts out with one courtier's remark: "Another fire. For whom hath it been lighted?/ A heretic—or a witch?" His companion replies: "I cannot say./ 'Tis not the fashion nowadays to worry" (148). In the dialogue between Emperor Rudolph and Kepler that follows we learn that the astronomer's mother is accused of witchcraft and that he himself is said to be "picking holes" in the dogmas of the Church (151). Hegel cites in the same context the cases of Copernicus and Galileo whose scientific genius was suppressed by the Catholic Church. Similarly, Kepler is ahead of his time and is longing for a period when the spirit of the people will be further developed and will have achieved greater freedom:

> Truth is a danger, terrible and deadly,
> Imparted to the People in our days.

The time will come—would it were here already—
When Truth will be discussed in ev'ry street.
But then—the People will have come of age! (188)

The parallel between the structural pattern of Madách's play and the dialectical progression as outlined by Hegel is noteworthy. The first stage of historical development, the Oriental world, can be considered the thesis. Adam as Pharaoh embodies its principle: All for One. Greek democracy presents the (first) antithesis: One (Adam as Miltiades) for All. But this principle is not yet universally applied. Slavery continues to exist in Rome, the second phase of the antithesis: Everybody for Himself. Madách seems to agree with Hegel that the Roman aristocracy is the worst form of society. Only Christianity provides the synthesis: Everybody for Everybody. Since all men are free now—at least the philosophical basis for slavery has been destroyed—this synthesis is far above the antithesis of Greek antiquity.

In complete agreement with Hegel's emphases Madách devotes one scene to the Orient, two to the classical age, and four to the Christian period which he, like Hegel, thus subdivides into consecutive phases. Each synthesis already contains the basis for a new opposing principle. The Constantinople scene, depicting the liberation of man through Christianity, also shows how that freedom is abolished.[21] Much space is allotted to the disagreements over doctrine and to the destruction of the initial unity of the new faith. Church and heretics confront each other with equal determination and assurance. Out of the original concept of everybody serving everybody, the new thesis develops: Collective against Collective. Kepler attempts to isolate himself from his society, but he has not yet reached the renewed and more profound freedom that the Reformation made possible. His antithesis, the escape into the seclusion of scientific endeavor, is doomed: The Individual against the Collective. The French Revolution brings the synthesis. The individual has now achieved new freedom by accepting the law of the new collective, the popular state. The motto is: Everybody for the Collective.

Madách goes beyond Hegel in dealing with his own time and even with the future as he imagines it. But the scenes that follow also conform to Hegel's dialectic scheme. Yet there is an important difference. Up to this point, Madách's dialectic—like that of Hegel—had a religious foundation. After the Paris scene it becomes secularized. Madách seems to move closer to Marx than to Hegel. The focus is no longer on individual consciousness but rather on societal structure.

The first modern social revolution had "elevated" the freedom of Christianity to a new plane. Now this synthesis becomes the new thesis: society, for whose liberty the individual—Danton—had fought, becomes an incited mob that crushes him. It is now the masses against the individual (but also against outdated class concepts). Equality for all turns into terror toward the individual. The antithesis is found in capitalism which abolishes equality through economic differentiation. Social inequality leads to the despotism of those who possess against those who depend. Order is conceived as oppression, and the final consequence is: Everybody against Everybody. This is the London scene, the world that Madách saw as the result of increasing industrialization.

The solution of the social question, the possibility of an ideal society could only lie in the future. Madách's concept of the society to come is based on the Phalanstery idea of Charles Fourier and on certain thoughts taken from Adam Smith, Victor Considérant, and Plato. Social differences have disappeared, and each person works according to ability. Individuality is no longer tolerated. Through the destruction of the family unit, the last basis for a separate consciousness outside the state is being eliminated. The French Revolution had proclaimed freedom and equality for all. The age of free trade and industrialization had abolished equality and consequently also freedom. The Phalanstery now establishes equality as the highest principle at the expense of individual freedom. But only "anachronistic" men sense that something is missing. The new synthesis is: The Collective for Everybody.

Madách's dialectic system leads to a conclusion quite different from that of Hegel. This is due to his pessimistic view of history, which was partly a consequence of what he had witnessed during his lifetime. With the Phalanstery scene the dialectic development of history comes to an end. While the message of the final visions can hardly be called positive, it should not be overlooked that Madách's drama as a whole presents a dialectic progression, too. The poet deals with the universal theme of the relationship between God and mankind, not only with the course of human history. On this higher plane, a development in three stages can also be observed.

The thesis is the original unity of God and man. In Eden Adam and Eve live in the assurance of harmony with the Creator. Lucifer's appearance introduces the antithesis. The first humans become aware of evil which they had not known before. Adam senses the presence of a destructive force: "Ah, woman! What was that unwonted sound?/ It seem'd as though some strange and hostile power / Had broken in upon our peace" (28). Man's fall means his separation from God. By himself, he tries to set his own goals. Innocent ignorance has given way to knowledge through guilt. But that process is also an awakening of consciousness. When Lucifer asks, "Are ye disheartened?" Adam retorts, "Nay. Not so!/ I do but shudder as I reawaken!" (39). The visions of history add only details to this antithesis but do not change its essence. As Adam becomes increasingly doubtful of his own strength, the synthesis is being prepared: at the end there is the return to the unity with God. After his odyssey through time, man recognizes that true freedom lies in the acceptance of bonds—an idea strongly emphasized by Hegel. The reunion with God means voluntary submission under divine law. The angelic choir praises this new and deeper freedom: "Freely betwixt Sin and Virtue / We can choose—this thought is grand" (299).

Hegel saw the meaning of history in the gradual awareness of this liberty. If the past is reviewed from this position, there is no meaninglessness in the historical development, and the study of the annals of mankind has become a theodicy. That, despite all pessimism, is also the deeper meaning of *Az ember tragédiája.*

Hegel and Madách agree that each synthesis contains the seeds for what will become a new antithesis. But Hegel applies his system only to the past and is careful not to make any predictions about future development. He does not regard his own period as ideal; nevertheless he views it as the hitherto highest stage. All that has happened is the result of divine planning, but it would be presumptuous to forecast God's intentions for the future. When Marx adopted Hegel's dialectic mechanism, he replaced the concept of "Spirit" with that of matter and thus eliminated the metaphysical foundation. Now the entire development is exclusively oriented toward the future. The phases of history do not follow any divine plan; instead, everything happens consistently and almost as if according to an unalterable law of nature. Eventually, there will be the perfect stage of complete happiness for all. After this highest stage—the classless society—no antithesis will be possible.

Madách's position, then, is somewhere between Hegel and Marx. It is unlikely that he was familiar with the work of the latter. Even though the *Communist Manifesto* had been translated into Hungarian almost immediately after its first publication, it failed to have much impact until sometime in the 1870s. But Madách, like Marx, attempts to predict future development, and he also places major emphasis on societal structure. What separates him from Marx is his negative view of the society of the future and his Hegelian interpretation of history as theodicy. Yet, for a Hungarian writer after 1848–49 it had become impossible to see his own epoch as the highest point of development. Madách is equally far from Hegel's apotheosis of the contemporary Prussian state and from Marx's faith in future perfection.

Some Hungarian scholars have studied Hegel's impact on Madách. Voinovich points to parallels in content and structure.[22] An article by Andor Sas deals with the relationship between the German philosopher and the Hungarian poet, and Riedl discusses briefly Hegel's dialectic system as it applies to Madách. He states that Hegel's philosophy of history was the prevalent view at the time when Madách wrote his drama.[23] More recently, however, this position has been challenged. Based on the fact that Madách does not mention Hegel in his letters and on the parodistic use of Hegelian terminology in *A civilizátor*, some critics have disputed the poet's knowledge of or interest in Hegel's philosophy. József Waldapfel claims in the introduction to his edition of *Az ember tragédiája* that the dialectic of the dream visions had sprung from the social contradictions in Madách's own epoch which was marked by the discrepancy between slogans of civic freedom and capitalistic reality. This was the main concern of the writer who derived the dialectic structure of his play from the study of his own age, not from reading Hegel.[24] Károly Horváth basically agrees with Waldapfel but adds that through Hegel the concept of a development through contradictions had become popular. Without it, Madách would hardly have selected this particular structural principle.[25]

Sőtér strongly rejects all claims of Hegel's impact. The irony in *A civilizátor* proves that Madách could not have been influenced by Hegel. In general, Sőtér sees the elevation of Madách to the position of a "philosopher" by earlier scholars as unwarranted.[26] However, Madách's satire is not directed against Hegel but rather against the Austrian Bach regime and its representative, the "civilizer" Stroom who wants to bring "Germanic-Christian" culture to the Hungarian barbarians. His pseudo-intellectualism as manifested in his inane mouthing of Hegelian slogans is ridiculed, not Hegel's philosophical approach to history. Of course, Béla Pukánszky is right in denouncing the notion that Madách had merely dramatized Hegel; whatever he took from the German work was organically incorporated into his literary masterpiece.[27] On the other hand, it is difficult to review the

Hegel parallels in *Az ember tragédiája* without concluding that the
Hungarian author arrived at his concept of historic development at
least partly as the result of his critical reading of *The Philosophy of
History*.

In an essay on Shakespeare Goethe stated that the plays of the English bard all had as their center that "mysterious point . . . where
the peculiarity of our individualism, the pretended freedom of our
will collides with the necessary course of the whole." [28] This "mysterious point" is also the center of Madách's drama of history which
depicts the struggle of man's individuality and its need for freedom
against a more-than-individual fate already traced out for him. Personal concern and historic necessity are the two poles that determine
Adam's thoughts and deeds.

This is also the point where individual tragedy and the course of
human history merge. In the framework of Madách's play history and
personal fate are not seen as independent of each other. There can be
no fulfillment in the encounters between Adam and Eve in the historic scenes. A personal relationship would mean the abandonment of
the Faustian principle. In his role as a "World-Historic Personality,"
Adam may not strive for personal happiness but has to try to push
mankind ahead. The fact that he realizes again and again the relativ-
ity of such progress and the insufficiency of man is tragic in a more
profound sense than the merely sad impossibility of establishing permanent human ties. This is the insight Lucifer wants to force on him:
there is very little, if any, true progress, and humanity does not really
change. Madách intends to show the tragedy of the individual, Adam,
as imbedded in the tragedy of mankind, in history. Adam accepts the
reality of each historical situation he enters. The fact that he has the
opportunity to move on to a different epoch does not change that
reality.

Thus, the historical panorama and Adam's tragedy form an insepa-
rable unity. History ends in nothingness: after some apparent progress mankind will revert to the stage of ferocious animals if conditions
of life deteriorate. Man has remained the same through the ages, only
the forms of society have changed as the result of differing ideals.
This realization leads to Adam's decision to commit suicide. His despair does not end when he learns that—due to Eve's pregnancy—
killing himself would be senseless. Neither the tragedy of mankind
nor the fate of the individual can come to a clearly positive conclusion in this world. Without denying the freedom of will, Madách sees

the final decisions as being made on a higher plane. Only there, the "Tragedy of Man" can become "Divine Comedy."

III   *Beyond the Human Sphere: The Metaphysical Framework*

The opening scene and the end of *Az ember tragédiája* constitute an extrahuman frame for the fall of man, the expulsion from Eden, and Adam's long journey through time. Writers from the Book of Job to modern times have been fascinated by this motif: man as the center of the struggle between God and Satan. This contest is the basis for Adam's tragedy and for the visions of history. There is little question about the outcome. The Book of Job, medieval mystery plays and Jesuit dramas, Pedro Calderón de la Barca, John Milton, Friedrich Gottlieb Klopstock, Gotthold Ephraim Lessing, and Johann Wolfgang von Goethe all agree that God must remain victorious. But neither Job nor Faust nor Adam is aware of this conclusion.

By tying world events to this metaphysical struggle, Madách follows Saint Augustine who saw history as resulting from man's defection from the Lord. Original sin established the worldly community, oriented toward man rather than God. Through his desire to be as God and to usurp divine powers, man falls prey to Satan. Only God's grace, embodied in Christ, can bring salvation and peace to humanity.

Az ember tragédiája is Madách's philosophical and religious credo. The drama presents the result and the chronicle of his evaluation of traditional and contemporary thought. In his attempt to define man's position in the universe, he wrestled with the concepts of popular materialism which were widely discussed at the time. His purchase of Ludwig Feuerbach's controversial *Essence of Christianity* is indicative of his interest.[29] Traces of this book can be found in the drama.

In his preface Feuerbach speaks in terms to be repeated almost verbatim by Madách's Kepler about the happier future when scholars and scientists will no longer have to be afraid to proclaim the truth. Truth never originates "in the splendor of thrones" but in obscurity. Those in high positions are never reached by the waves of world history, only those in low places.[30] Lucifer argues similarly when he states that from the battlements of the London Tower, the "rushing tide of life" may seem like a "pious anthem," but that below it sounds differently (195). Pharaoh could not hear the anguished cries of his slaves, and Adam is still misjudging life from an equally lofty station,

just as history "scans and weighs the vanished past" without record-
ing the misery of the common people (197).

Lucifer serves as Feuerbach's spokesman throughout the play. In
trying to persuade Adam to break God's law, he echoes the philosopher's views on the essential difference between man and animal.
Consciousness, the power of thought as the "light of the intellect,"
sets man apart from the rest of nature. The consciousness of a cater-
pillar does not extend beyond the species of plant to which its life is
confined.[31] Lucifer makes the identical point: "the tiny maggot," eat-
ing away the fruit before Adam's mouth, may imagine being conscious, but in the human soul a wider consciousness is "dawning already" (32–33). When Adam expresses impatience because he has not
eaten of the Tree of Life, he is reminded that "all things that live,
endure for the same span," the century-old tree and the short-lived
mayfly experience life, growth, and death alike (50). Feuerbach had
said that, to the ephemera, its brief lifespan means the same as many
years of life to another being.[32]

Additional parallels could be listed to show Madách's use of ideas
and formulations from the German work. But more important is a
look at his general attitude toward its materialistic monism. Feuerbach's system is man-centered and relies on tangible reality, not on
abstract thought or unprovable hypotheses. Man can only comprehend his own concrete being, and his concept of God is directly related to it: "Consciousness of God is man's self-consciousness, knowledge of God is man's self-knowledge." [33] God is then identical with
man's own being, freed from the bonds of the individual. He is man,
made objective, viewed and revered as a separate being. Man is the
beginning, the center, and the end of all religion. Theology thus becomes anthropology; there is no longer any difference between this
world and the hereafter, and man can fully concentrate on the present.

The last of Madách's dream visions hints at this identity of the human and the divine that makes man the creator of his own deity.
Adam voices indignation over the sacrifice with which the Eskimo
tries to pacify his gods, and Lucifer sneers:

> Wast thou not even so?
> The only difference between you two
> Is this . . . his seal he offers to his god,
> While thou didst sacrifice Mankind to thine,
> That each of you had made in his own image! (281–82)

The fact that it is again Lucifer who represents Feuerbach indicates Madách's position. For the poet, God is a real and acting power outside the human sphere, not man's self-reflection. Certainly this concept was not merely dictated by the requirements of the stage which might account for the specific traits of the Lord as a *dramatis persona*. To Madách, the reality of God is the prerequisite for a positive solution. Without it, Adam's striving would become totally meaningless, and the final message would be the nihilism of the Eskimo scene.

Pessimism and materialism can be overcome by the faith demanded in the final scene. Feuerbach had tried to reduce religion to the human level. Madách shows instead man's return to God. The ideal religion is the active and pure faith proclaimed by Saint Peter and Tancred. Man's position in Madách's world view is very different from that outlined by Feuerbach. This is emphasized by the concluding angelic choir: God in His power does not need us to execute His plans, but in His goodness, He allows us to participate in His great design:

> But on thy high path thou'lt never
> By the proud thought blinded be
> That what thou dost for God's glory,
> Is expressly done by thee,
> As if in thy Maker's actions
> Thou a lawful share mightst claim—
> 'Tis a free gift if He bids thee
> Do aught for His sovereign aim. (300)

Thus Madách rejects Feuerbach and affirms his faith in God.

Madách's study of another leading exponent of popular materialism leads to a similar—if somewhat more complex—position. The poet was a keen observer of scientific developments. He owned Humboldt's *Cosmos* and quoted from it when addressing the Kisfaludy Society; he referred to Jakob Moleschott's scientific materialism in his notes; and allusions in *Az ember tragédiája* attest to his familiarity with recent scientific theories. He probably knew about the 1854 Göttingen convention of scientists and physicians which marked the climax in the debate between the representatives of idealism and of materialism. Ludwig Büchner's *Force and Matter* of 1855 was a tangible result of this debate.

Büchner's very successful book is a popular summary of the basic ideas of materialism. The author tried to demonstrate through many examples that our universe was not created or maintained by any divine power. The world of matter is infinite and is subject only to the inherent laws of nature. There is no force outside matter. The concepts of God as creator, of individual life after death, or of true freedom of will are fantasies. The difference between man and beast is quantitative: both are merely specific arrangements of matter.

Although *Force and Matter* is not listed among Madách's books, it can be assumed that he knew it since numerous passages in his drama seem based on its examples.[34] The very title of the book is mockingly quoted by Lucifer when Adam as Pharaoh feels strongly attracted to Eve and asks how man can resist such elementary force: "Why, there would seem no way out, but for Knowledge / To swear this hidden thread does not exist,/ While Strength and Matter rudely laugh at it" (58).[35]

In the third scene Lucifer points out—as examples for apparently aimless individuals—the "ants and swarming bees" that act purposefully in a general plan (50–51). Büchner uses the identical image when discussing animal intelligence. On three occasions Büchner mentions the intestinal worm that needs the bodies of different animals for its various stages of development. In the last scene of Madách's play Lucifer reminds Adam of the "parasite" he once studied "which only can exist / In cats and hawks, although, at first, it cannot / Develop save in th'entrails of a mouse" (291). In the same context Lucifer mentions the statistical regularity of suicides and madness (292), an example that comes directly from Büchner's book where it is similarly used as an argument against the notion of a free will. Büchner's description of the Arctic North and its people and his reference to the "heaven of the Greenlanders which represents their greatest wish for a rich superabundance of blubber and fish" [36] are echoed in Madách's penultimate scene where Lucifer also expresses Büchner's view that man and animal are the same:

> Try as thou wilt to cheat thyself,
> Thou must obey the animal within thee.
> And not until its appetite is stilled
> Will what is Man in thee look down with scorn
> Upon the first essential of his being. (283)

Büchner's system has no room for the concept of a divine creator. Since the laws of nature are absolute, they would have to apply even to a god who first established them. Büchner sarcastically attacks traditional religion in pointing to the rather low opinion people must have of their self-created god who could be moved by prayers and sighs to overturn the indestructible order he himself had set up, to interfere with the perfect functioning of nature's mechanism.[37] Lucifer, in obvious agreement, refuses to join the adoring angels in their praise of the Lord. He also emphasizes the laws and the force inherent in matter:

> Why should it please me? Is't because dead matter
> Hath been by Thee informed with attributes
> Whereof, unless they had themselves revealed,
> Thou never, maybe, wouldst have dreamt or known,
> Nor, hadst Thou dreamt of them, couldst have compelled
> To change, obedient to Thy purposes? (20–21)

He then proceeds to forecast the experiment of the scientist in the Phalanstery: "Soon, too, if Man should e'er divine Thy methods,/ He will attempt to do what Thou hast done" (21).

This motif, the creation of artificial life in the laboratory, is often seen as inspired by the Homunculus episode in Goethe's *Faust*. But Büchner, too, is a likely source. He tried to show the absurdity of the concept of a "Vital Force" unrelated to matter. Proponents of that idea stress the failure of chemists to create organic compounds from inorganic substances. If there were no such life-giving force, it should be possible to manufacture human beings in the retort. In response, Büchner refers to the successful creation of artificial organic compounds. His outlook is entirely optimistic, and he sees no reason to doubt "even the most marvelous possibilities." [38] Madách's scientist voices the same belief: "The secret of our own organic life / At any moment now we may discover" (251).

If living organisms are merely systems of chemical processes, then death is but a rearrangement of permanent matter. Büchner emphasizes that nothing can disappear in such transformation: "Matter is immortal, indestructible; not a particle of dust in the universe, no matter how small or large, can be lost, none can be added . . . . The body in its individual form is mortal, to be sure, but not in its component parts." [39] The chorus of the London scene makes the same point: "Nothing in the world is wasted./ What is new, of old we tasted" (195), and Lucifer assures Adam: "Thy body, true, may crumble into dust / But in unnumbered shapes 'twill be revived" (51).

In his flight through space Adam tries to cut his ties to the material world. The voice of the Earth Spirit reminds him that his life is possible only through those bonds. But Adam defies him and sides with idealism in its rejection of the primacy of matter: "My body may be thine—my soul is mine!/ For Thought and Truth I know are infinite!/ They were long, long before thy world of Matter!" (270). The Spirit's response is an unequivocal affirmation of Büchner's position:

> Does aroma come before the rose,
> Form before body, light before the sun?
>
> . . . .
>
> For all thou dost feel,
> All thou dost understand, is the result
> Of emanations of that mass of Matter
> Thou namest Earth. And were it otherwise,
> It could no more exist, nor couldst thou be. (271)

These and numerous other parallels indicate that Büchner's work served as one of Madách's most significant sources in the area of natural science and natural philosophy. But *Az ember tragédiája* also shows that he did not accept its message uncritically. As with Feuerbach, most of Büchner's materialistic arguments Lucifer voices as part of his plan to mislead or destroy mankind. We may not, however, interpret him simply as being the symbol of matter. He refers to his own spirituality when commenting on the bond between man and nature: "That is the only thing that dare defy me,/ Because it is a Spirit, like myself" (43). Lucifer uses the ideas of materialism to convince Adam, the representative of naive idealism, that ideals are mere self-deception. Yet when during their space flight Lucifer expounds on the absurdity of all human goals, Adam nevertheless vows to continue the struggle for principles which—despite their dubiousness and temporariness—move mankind forward. This is the moment when the decision is made against Büchner and for Hegel. Adam is not swayed by the historical examples Lucifer cites in the Eskimo scene to show how everything great and noble is relative, depends on accident, and is based on material conditions. He has remained an idealist who rejects the paralyzing consequences of a materialistic and mechanistic interpretation of the world. Presumably speaking for the poet himself, he says:

> Ah, say no more! All that thou hast unfolded
> Seems to be true and simple. And, for that,

> It is so much more deadly. Only fools
> Are blinded by mere Superstition. They,
> Thou seest, are unable to perceive the Spirit
> Which prompts us and which acts upon us all.
> A good man, none the less, would recognize
> His brother, if thy cold doctrine did not kill him. (285)

Sőtér states correctly that "in the final analysis, Madách rejects the materialistic viewpoint—but his temporary agreement with Lucifer's positions attests to the fact that he reached this rejection only after an intensive inner debate." [40]

Yet Madách's rejection of materialism is not unequivocal. Lucifer is an exponent of materialistic ideas, to be sure, but so is the Earth Spirit. Unlike Lucifer, he stood among the angels who praised the Lord of Creation. Thus, the initial positions are quite different: the materialism of the Spirit of the Earth is only apparently akin to that of Büchner. Lucifer emphasizes the autonomy of matter and questions God's eternity and power; the Earth Spirit understands himself as part of the divine creation. He does not raise matter to the position of supreme importance but rather embodies man's innate ties to the earth. God has established limitations that may not be disregarded. If man attempts to leave his natural realm, even the positive material force can no longer sustain him.

The Phalanstery scene shows most clearly how the Earth Spirit serves as a counterbalance to absolute materialism. The third scene had already demonstrated the superiority of the positive forces of nature over Lucifer's negation. Now the Spirit of the Earth confronts human arrogance in its attempt to imitate the miracle of creation. Here Madách rejects Büchner's optimistic view: the scientist, mockingly called "Nature's stoker" by Lucifer, does not succeed because of a "stupid accident," as he sees it. But the poet indicates that this failure is not accidental. Man may not cross the limit set by God. As the scientist claims that only one more step separates him from the final triumph, Adam replies:

> But he who has not made that final step
> Has nothing done, and still is ignorant.
> The other steps were taken in the courtyard;
> The last should lead to the most holy secret.
> Oh, will that final step be ever taken? (254)

The Earth Spirit's "No" to this question is Madách's final answer to Büchner and popular materialism.

Madách apparently takes a dualistic approach to the material world. He distinguishes between two spheres of matter. Lucifer's power is based on one. The two trees in Eden are real and provide a starting point for him. He can call on the elements for help in his effort to lead man astray. He can make nature's forces visible and can even conjure up the Spirit of the Earth. But he cannot control him who embodies the other, positive aspect of matter. The helpful forces of nature are everywhere, ready to serve man who can find them "dispersed in water, clouds and mist and groves,/ Wherever he might chance to turn his eyes / With ardent longing and aspiring soul" (48). In a way, the possibility of a positive solution of man's tragedy is also based on this Earth Spirit concept: Eve's pregnancy is the victory of the most profound force of nature. Only after this power has defeated the spirit of negativity does the Lord call for confidence and hope.

Through the study of Feuerbach and Büchner Madách came to his own assessment of nature. The premise of a purely material universe leads to nihilism. Harmony is possible only by recognizing the divine idea as well as nature's positive forces. Madách did not deny the importance of matter. He rejected both pure materialism and abstract idealism that ignores facts. He felt close to Humboldt in this position. But Madách did not arrive at a unified world view. The assumption of two different realms of nature is hardly a satisfactory solution. Sőtér may be right in arguing that certain passages in *Az ember tragédiája* are difficult to interpret because Madách did not think all philosophical questions through to their logical conclusion.[41]

Madách's religious and philosophical views have been assailed repeatedly. Catholic reviewers especially often objected to his "atheism" and "slanderous attacks on Christianity." János Dudek, an early critic, saw Madách's position as dangerous and destructive and called the play a "Bible for prospective suicides." The drama's success was the result of its nihilism which corresponded to the *Zeitgeist*. Moreover, the positive reactions of Arany or Szász were not based on critical judgment: they simply rushed to the aid of a fellow Protestant.[42] While Dudek's argument merits little serious attention, the erroneous designation of Madách as a Protestant persists.

Some critics took issue with the "religious caricature" in the Constantinople scene by an author with so little understanding of Christian teachings that he considered the all-important question of the divinity of Jesus a quarrel over one Greek letter. Madách's motivation in portraying the corruption of the Church was overlooked or misinterpreted, as was his introduction of positive Christian models. Occasionally, his representation of the Lord was also attacked as disrespectful.

More important are those critical views that concentrated on Madách's message and not on details. The Jesuit Jakob Overmans and similarly the Bishop of Székesfehérvár, Ottokár Prohászka, deplored his pessimism that paved the way for a dangerous nihilism. Because of his lack of faith, the playwright was just as incapable of providing spiritual guidance as Goethe had been. The Lord's final admonition is incongruous since it is not based on anything in the poem itself.[43] Overmans specifically objected to the Kantian ethics of the last scene. God should have provided Adam with an answer about the future in order to bring out the best in man.[44]

Madách owned Immanuel Kant's *Critique of Pure Reason*. But it would be difficult to show many direct parallels, since the intentions of the German philosopher were so different. Only where Kant touches on problems of "practical reason" can we see some possible impact. The three basic questions Kant raises are the same that Adam asks after his dream visions: "What can I know? What ought I to do? What may I hope?" [45] God does not provide clear and positive answers, however. Kant suggests: "The ultimate aim to which the speculation of reason in its transcendental employment is directed concerns three objects: the freedom of the will, the immortality of the soul, and the existence of God." [46] God's existence is never questioned in the Hungarian drama—at least not in practical terms, since Madách has the Lord appear on stage. Kant's postulate of freedom of will, on the other hand, is of major importance for Adam. Through all the dismal visions of history he wants to retain his belief that he can make his own decisions while Lucifer tries to convince him that such freedom is an illusion: " 'Tis Fate dictates the hist'ry of the world:/ Thou art its tool, and driven as it wills." Adam refuses to accept that: "Not so. Thou liest! For this my will is free!" (290). And the final angelic choir assures man that he has indeed a free choice. Madách, like Kant, sees this freedom as the prerequisite for ethical action.

But Adam does not receive an answer to the third question: "Ah, tell me, tell me now what fate awaits me . . ./ Is all that I can hope this brief existence?" Instead of affirming that he will live on, the Lord directs his attention to man's sphere of action: "Strong is thine arm, and upright is thy heart./ An endless field invites thee now to work" (296, 298). This turn toward the practical is found in Kant in the same context: "If, then, these three cardinal propositions are not in any way necessary for *knowledge*, and are yet strongly recommended by our reason, their importance, properly regarded, must concern only the *practical*. . . . The three above-mentioned problems . . . however . . . refer us yet further, namely to the problem *what we ought to do*, if the will is free, if there is a God and a future world." [47]

Kant's *Critique of Practical Reason* carries this thought further, and the moral philosophy he outlines here provides a basis for the Lord's refusal to give clear responses to Adam's questions. This uncertainty is the source of greatness and virtue. Ethical action should spring from the inner moral code without regard to compensation in this world or the next. The greatness inherent in virtue and the happy knowledge of one's noble deeds are reward enough. This idealistic view is of course refuted in Büchner's materialistic philosophy which denies that man can be good for the sake of goodness. So the final scene amounts to another repudiation of popular materialism by Madách.

While Kant asserts that the questions of freedom of will, immortality, or the existence of God cannot be answered by speculative reason, they are most meaningful in the realm of practical reason. If we had final assurance, our actions would be governed by fear or hope, not by the innate feeling of duty. The Lord in Madách's drama seems to agree with Kant that this certainty would decrease the moral value of our action:

> Oh, seek not
> To probe the secret that God's kindly hand
> Hath wisely hidden from thy yearning eyes.
> For, shouldst thou see that, on the Earth, thy soul
> Stays but a while, and, yonder, lives for ever,
> Thy suff'ring would no longer be a virtue.
> And, shouldst thou see thy soul absorb'd in dust,
> What would there be to spur thy high ideals? (297)

As in Kant, this uncertainty is seen as a gift to mankind. And the "moral law within" which, according to the philosopher, fills "the mind with ever new and increasing admiration and awe," lies within man and does not come from the outside.[48] This is the inner voice to which God refers Adam: "And, if thou listenst, thou shalt hear a voice / That ne'er will fail to warn and to uplift thee./ Obey that voice!" (298–99). The angelic choir reaffirms the idea that noble deeds carry their own reward:

> Act then boldly, never caring
> If thou findst ingratitude;
> Not thanks—self-esteem shall govern
> Him who does aught great and good.
> Shame's the spur of noble actions,
> And the conscience of this shame,
> While discouraging the coward,
> Gives the brave the loftiest aim. (300)

The discussion of Kant's ethics leads to a question of great importance for the interpretation of *Az ember tragédiája:* what is the position of evil in Madách's world view? The first scene seems to conform to traditional Christian teachings. Lucifer, who had served as one of the archangels, rebels and is banished. But his attitude indicates that his relationship to God is more complicated. He does not join in the adoration of the other angels because of his special position:

> That wretched legion gives Thee praise enough.
> And rightly, too—to praise Thee is its duty!
> Thy Light conceived those Shadows there. But I
> Have been since the beginning here on high! (22)

His role as archangel was apparently only a temporary mask for his basic negativity. This negativity, he asserts, provided the incentive for the Lord's creation of the universe. He demands his share of what they thus jointly created. As death is eternally linked to life, he has always existed with God and they will continue to coexist. From this vantage point it would be absurd to praise God as the ultimate power: "Wherever Thou art, there, behold, am I./ And, knowing Thee so well, am I to kneel?" (23). Even though the Lord states in response that he could utterly destroy Lucifer, he does not refute his claims.

Thus, Madách presents a dualistic relationship between God and the Devil. Even as—seemingly in accordance with the biblical account—the Lord surveys his completed work, judges it good, and desires to rest, his very words indicate that there is an opposing principle against which he must give protection:

> The wheels go round, and the Creator rests.
> Ages may pass before I shall renew
> One spoke that Time may weaken with its tests.
> Rise then, ye guardian Angels of My world—
> Bestir yourselves, begin your endless flight! (18)

The struggle between the opposing principles seems perpetual, and God's triumphs only temporal. This is clearly expressed by Lucifer: "I must forever by Thy might be vanquished,/ Forever I am doom'd to lose my battles—/ But always to renew the fight, refreshed" (23). He is no longer the Devil of Christian tradition but truly the concept of eternal negation. His function as outlined here— and not contradicted by the Lord—reflects a dualism that corresponds to Persian Zoroastrianism or Manichaeism. It is surprising that Madách's Catholic critics, while objecting to Lucifer's arrogant tone, apparently overlooked this basic deviation from Christian dogma. Good and evil are locked in eternal battle; neither can completely destroy the other; both seem subject to an even higher, indefinite power that limits them.

The parallel with Persian myth may not be accidental. Hegel had dealt in great detail with the dualism of Ormuzd, the Lord of the "Kingdom of Light," and Ahriman, the representative of darkness. According to Hegel, "the harmonizing of the contradiction is only that Ormuzd shall defeat Ahriman, but yet eternally fight him." [49] This is the situation Lucifer describes.

But Lucifer is unable to destroy man spiritually (or physically, as his original plan has failed) and thus loses his fight against the Lord. In the course of the drama his relationship to God—and Madách's own position on the function of evil—undergoes a fundamental change. The Lord's initial claim that he could destroy his opponent had appeared unfounded. In the final scene, however, Lucifer is clearly inferior to the Lord who emerges with the authority of the absolute ruler: "O, Spirit! Down i' the dust!/ Before Me none is great!" (295). Lucifer cannot "crawl away" as the voice of God commands him to stay and listen to the description of the part he is to play henceforth:

> Thou, also, Lucifer, art still a link
> Essential to My Universe. Live on!
> Thy chilling knowledge, thy inept denials,
> Will be the leaven that will make thee work.
> And, though for a brief spell it may beguile

> Man from his course, it will not greatly matter.
> Ere long Man will return to me again.
> But thy chastisement will be infinite!
> Forever thou wilt see what thou wouldst kill
> Become new germs of Beauty and of Glory! (299)

This idea of the ultimately positive role of absolute evil in God's plans is a key element in Goethe's *Faust*. But it goes back to Saint Augustine whose path Madách retraced in his change of position. Augustine had originally embraced the Manichaean concept of the universe, largely shaped by Zoroastrian thought. Only after a long struggle had he accepted the Christian view and forcefully opposed Manichaeism. In the last scene of his play Madách, too, rejects a dualistic world view and embraces Christian concepts. His Lucifer, who had rebelled against God in the confidence of his own power, has now become a tool of goodness.

Adam's salvation is related to this change in Madách's metaphysical system. Original sin, man's desertion of his Creator, had resulted for Adam and mankind in the loss of divine grace. Man's sinfulness broke his original close tie to God, and the chance once provided is gone. Yet God is ready to restore His grace to repenting man. But, as Hegel suggested, the synthesis fundamentally differs from the original thesis: Eden remains lost. In contrast to Byron's heroes or to Faust, Adam fulfills an important prerequisite—according to Catholic doctrine—that makes him worthy of God's grace. True, he had been on the verge of committing mortal sin by trying to take his own life, but he ultimately recognizes in Eve's motherhood the power of God which forces him to repent and to realize his own weakness: "Lord, Thou hast conquered! See, I'm in the dust!/ In vain I strove, without Thee, and against Thee!/ Raise me, or crush me, now . . . I bare my breast" (294). This insight makes his salvation possible. The Council of Trent had affirmed as dogma that the sinner can attain absolution only in two steps: preparation for absolution, and absolution itself. He has to have faith in the truth of salvation, has to have fear, hope, love, and repentance. Faith is the foundation. This does not constitute any right to divine grace on the part of man but makes him receptive to God's forgiveness which is freely given and not owed.

The Lord's final words underscore his promise of grace. Despite the visions, whose message is not denied, Adam can confidently face life's struggle in the knowledge of God's restored favor. Only in this way can he find the strength to live on. This Christian view of salva-

tion is further emphasized in Eve's reference to a future "Child of
Sorrow" who will wash away sin and misery and will fill the world
with brotherhood (295). Adam can live in this hope even without ob-
taining final certainty.

It is hard to see how Madách's message could be termed "nihilis-
tic." His drama does not end in the barren loneliness of the ice region
but with man and God reunited. This final scene marks the essential
difference between his position and that of Mark Twain's posthumous
story "The Mysterious Stranger" which offers some remarkable parallels to the Hungarian play. Twain's protagonist Theodor Fischer,
growing up in sixteenth-century Austria, meets Satan, the fallen
angel, who leads him through different countries to show him the
misery of mankind. Whether in France or China, there is only oppression and despotism; and superstition triumphs in the name of the
Church. Innocent people fall victim to witch hunts. In a series of visions Satan reveals to Theodor the history of humanity: "Would you
like to see a history of the progress of the human race?—its development of that product it calls civilization?" [50]

Satan's survey of history begins with the slaying of Abel; other
biblical scenes of depravity and destruction follow. War seems to be
the dominant element in the history to come: Egyptians, Greeks, and
Romans fight and kill; and Christianity does not bring an end to the
bloodshed. Misery and murder persist. Even the future that Satan dis-
closes presents the same sad spectacle. Satan's frequent ironic comments try to demonstrate the futility of everything human: " 'And
what does it amount to?' said Satan, with his evil chuckle. 'Nothing at
all. You gain nothing; you always come out where you went in. For a
million years the race has gone on monotonously propagating itself
and monotonously reperforming this dull nonsense—to what end? No
wisdom can guess!' " [51] The similarity with Lucifer's visions of history and his intentions is obvious.

After Satan has led Theodor around for a year, he returns to the
nothingness from where he had come. His final words are the essence
of nihilism: *"Life itself is only a vision, a dream. . . . Nothing* exists;
all is a dream. God—man—the world—the sun, the moon, the wilder-
ness of stars—a dream, all a dream; they have no existence. *Nothing
exists save empty space—and you!"* With biting sarcasm, he proceeds
to outline the inconsistencies in religious beliefs: an almighty God
who nevertheless creates evil men, who burdens them with the responsibility for their actions, and who forces them into adoration is
but a meaningless specter from a dream: "Nothing exists but you.

And you are but a *thought*—a vagrant thought, a useless thought, a homeless thought, wandering forlorn among empty eternities!" [52] This would have been Adam's fate if Lucifer had succeeded in space.

A separate look at the three levels of action of Madách's drama was necessary in order to examine his intentions. Now it is important to focus on its unity which emerges as its author's credo. Individual tragedy and visions of history proved to be interwoven. Yet history and personal fate become meaningful only in relation to the third level, the extrahuman frame.

The external unity, determining the structure of the drama, is marked by the simple superimposition of the three levels discussed. The foundation for the entire work is the metaphysical conflict of the principles of good and evil. It ends with the total defeat of the negative force. This power struggle necessitates the second level: Lucifer uses Adam—individual and representative of humanity—as his pawn. He is to become the basis of his anti-divine empire. This plan, which he begins to realize by manipulating man's fall in Eden, eventually fails. The instrument he unsuccessfully employs to destroy man's spirit is the third level, the visions of history designed to lead to nihilism. Although Madách's letter to Erdélyi stresses human progress, the final vision is that of the icy wasteland.

Lucifer plays a specific role on each level. On the one hand, he is God's opponent. On the other hand, he is Adam's guide and commentator on the journey through history. And he tries to lead Adam, the individual, to a defiance of God and eventually to suicide. Similarly, Adam's functions are different on the three levels. In the metaphysical framework he is—at least for Lucifer—merely a tool. In the historical scenes he is an active participant or passive observer. Outside the dream world he attempts to draw the conclusions from what he has seen. Here Eve provides the impetus for an inner change. She does not appear to have gone through similar experiences, and her naive affirmation of life makes salvation possible.

Thus, the three levels are inseparably linked through action and *dramatis personae*. The last scene integrates everything into final unity. Through the·reappearance of the Lord the extrahuman frame is taken up again, but now Adam's individual destiny and that of mankind are incorporated. God's admonition to strive on in confidence indicates his victory over the power of evil. It provides Adam, the individual, with new hope, enabling him to continue his existence. But these final words are also meant for humanity as a whole and imply that the nihilism of Lucifer cannot be the ultimate meaning of history. Since God does not give absolute certainty and does not erase the message of Lucifer's visions by declaring their author a deceiver, man's decision to trust and strive has much more meaning than a resolution based on definite knowledge. Adam has to choose freely between good and evil; the decision on a higher plane does not relieve him of that choice. Madách does not become a spokesman for predestination; he is neither Jansenist nor Calvinist.

Therefore, the words of the final angelic choir are not contradictory but mark the position that Madách—in agreement with basic teachings of Christianity—sees for man:

> Freely betwixt Sin and Virtue
> We can choose—this thought is grand;
> While we know that o'er us hovers
> Grace, a shield in God's own hand. (299–300)

For Madách, only faith can reconcile the apparent contradiction between free human decision and divine power and omniscience. The admonition to trust and strive signifies the final unity of the three levels of *Az ember tragédiája* and is the poet's own credo. Through confidence in God Madách overcame pessimism without, however, substituting shallow optimistic belief in the future. From the Manichaean dualism of the opening scene, by way of a tendency toward pantheism as symbolized by the Earth Spirit (and also expressed in some of his lyrical poetry), he arrived at the monotheism of Christianity, albeit free from dogmatic limitations.

CHAPTER 5

The "Hungarian Faust"? Madách and the Faust Tradition

I *Adam as a Faustian Hero*

A. S. C. WALLIS, the Dutch translator of Madách's drama, tried to define the literary prototype exemplified by Adam. After referring to Don Juan, the Wandering Jew, and Faust, she concluded that he is the combination of all three. Madách asks which of their extreme characteristics we can find in ourselves. This question translates into the more general query: What is man? What is his destiny? Is he just an instrument, or is he capable of independent action? In light of Madách's philosophical orientation, she stated flatly, "Madách's play is a Faust tragedy . . . the first man is already a Faust." [1]

Few themes in world literature have been treated more frequently and under more diverse aspects than the life of the notorious Doctor Johann Faust, German magician and necromancer of the sixteenth century. This colorful character caught the imagination of the early authors who fashioned the first chapbooks out of various legends, and of Christopher Marlowe who forged these popular accounts into an early dramatic masterpiece. Enlightenment and Storm and Stress, Romanticism and Biedermeier all had their versions of Faust's adventures, and modern writers like Paul Valéry and Thomas Mann used the Faust myth to discuss their own era. But most people associate Faust's name with the most profound work ever written about him, Goethe's drama, in which the Faustian concept is most fully developed.

Each era saw in Faust a reflection of its own concerns and treated his character accordingly. Emphasis was always placed on the extraordinary qualities of a man who cannot be gauged by traditional standards. Even when his negative aspects were condemned, a certain greatness in him seemed to demand respect and made him a tragic hero. This is particularly obvious in Marlowe who far surpasses his German models in this regard. Faust, not satisfied with the knowledge and limited experiences apportioned to him, rebels and seeks new pathways. Unrestrained inquisitiveness, restless searching, dissatisfaction with things as they are, but also lust for life and a drive for power are among his features. Gotthold Lessing, in the spirit of Enlightenment, would emphasize the thirst for knowledge, whereas Goethe, much closer to the earlier versions, stressed the totality of Faust's ambitions. Faust attempts to gain insights normally denied mankind, and his striving leads him into the arms of Satan. In his quest this heroic and titanic seeker is completely alone. No human commitment may interfere with his restless thrust.

While traditional religion viewed the effort to transcend man's limitations as sinful and deserving of eternal damnation, Lessing and Goethe permitted Faust to be saved because this very effort ennobles him. Without Faustian man there would be no progress for the human race. Thus, the modern concept of "Faustian" has acquired a meaning that goes far beyond the significance of the historical figure. The German-Hungarian poet Nikolaus Lenau rightly stated: "*Faust* was written by Goethe, to be sure, but is not therefore Goethe's monopoly to the exclusion of everybody else. This Faust is mankind's common property." [2] The authors of the German Storm and Stress period and of the European Romantic movement felt akin to this prototype and attempted again and again new treatments of the Faust theme.

Madách's Adam shares many of the characteristics outlined here, and his attitude is often strikingly similar to that of the other Romantic loners. Critic Heinrich Kalek, in discussing Hungarian plays on German stages, wrote about Madách:

He very consciously created a supranational drama of mankind, and he naturally had to orient himself by that great model, by Goethe's *Faust,* just as the no less original Byron had done. . . . When Madách, as so many others, entered into competition with Goethe and tried to outdo him with a bolder structure of ideas, he certainly hit upon the more ingenious idea than Grabbe, for instance, who attempted to surpass Goethe's *Faust* with the doubling of Faust and Don Juan.[3]

This assessment takes for granted Madách's acquaintance with Goethe's work and his intent to compete with it. Obviously, Arany had come to the same conclusion after reading the drama's first scene. Frequently the relationship to *Faust* has been overemphasized.

Madách has often been depicted as merely an imitator or a devoted disciple of Goethe. Perhaps it is natural that German reviewers have repeatedly stressed his alleged dependence on Goethe as a model. The first published reviews in German journals called *Az ember tragédiája* a "Hungarian Faustiad" and Madách "the Hungarian Faust author." [4] On the occasion of the 1892 Vienna performance a well-known critic claimed that Madách's entire way of thinking and feeling could be traced back to Goethe.[5] Of course, there are very clear parallels, both in general themes and in details. A Hungarian scholar, Vilma Pröhle, has listed forty-four literal correspondences, some of which are rather superficial.[6] But any student of both writers could add to that list. In general, Hungarian critics have played down connections between the two works. Ignác Kont, in his history of Hungarian literature, went as far as to refer to Madách's acquaintance with Humboldt without even mentioning Goethe.[7]

Madách knew at least one other version of the Faust legend: his library contained August Klingemann's *Faust,* a work of minor literary importance. In addition, his notes and his correspondence show that he had read some of the writings of Lessing, Lenau, and Heine. It is possible that he was familiar with their respective Faust poems. But only the similarities between his work and those of Goethe and Lessing are worthy of analysis.

There is no documentary evidence for Madách's acquaintance with Lessing's dramatic works. Tancred's confrontation with the Patriarch of Constantinople, the embodiment of religious intolerance, is reminiscent of Lessing's *Nathan the Wise.* And the strong plea for the acceptance of differing religious positions which Lessing made in his play would certainly have met with Madách's approval. But some parallels between basic concepts in *Az ember tragédiája* and in Lessing's fragments of a *Faust* drama are even more remarkable.

The most important sources for Lessing's plans are the completed scene he published in his *Letters Concerning the Most Recent German Literature* of 1759, an additional manuscript found in his estate, and a number of fairly detailed reports by his friends. In contrast to all earlier authors, Lessing was convinced that man should not be punished for his searching and striving. For all his errors and transgressions, Faust is a truth seeker and thus has to be saved. This is a completely new concept and a significant break with the Faust tradition: Lessing proposes salvation not only for a sinner but even for an unrepentant one. Faust's unquenchable thirst for knowledge, in the past considered the cause of his downfall, now becomes the justification for his salvation. When the legions of Hell believe they have won, the angel of the Lord exclaims: "Do not exult, you have not triumphed over humanity and knowledge; Divinity has not given to man the most noble of drives in order to make him eternally miserable!" [8] To make Faust's salvation possible despite his flagrant flouting of God's laws, Lessing employed a trick that recurs in Madách's drama in slightly modified form: Faust's seduction and damnation take place within a dream, the devils are deceived by means of a phantom, and Faust, upon awakening, has learned his lesson and will henceforth mend his ways.

Both Lessing and Madách had not primarily thought of creating works for the stage. Rather, the dramatic form was to serve them as a vehicle for the discussion of abstract questions, of philosophical or esthetic theses. Lessing wrote the first scene of his play as a contribution to the debate on the reform of the German theater of his period. Madách used his hero's experiences to define his own religious and philosophical views. But both pose the same basic question: Should man, pressed on by his desire for immediate knowledge, ultimately perish? In view of this parallel, Gyula Haraszti could justifiably call Madách's Adam "a brother of Lessing's Faust." [9] The two authors agreed that the Faustian individual should be saved. Yet for the Hungarian poet, in the wake of personal and national tragedy, it was much more difficult to decide on a positive conclusion than for the German writer imbued with the optimistic spirit of Enlightenment. Still, Eve's argument seems to echo the words of Lessing's angel:

> If God hath traced
> The road that we should follow, surely He
> Should have created us in such a way
> That we should have no wish to go astray! (37)

There is a fundamental difference, however. What had been the divine motivation for the redemption of searching man is now Eve's attempt to justify her disregard of God's rule.

The two authors see the spiritual and moral destruction of man as more important than his physical annihilation. Their representatives of evil try to utilize the heroes' intellectual curiosity for this purpose. Lessing's devil explains that "too much inquisitiveness is a fault; and from one fault, all vices can spring if one indulges in it too much." [10] In *Az ember tragédiája* Lucifer wants to implant in the first human beings a desire for divine knowledge so that they will fall prey to him all the easier. In a Lessing fragment Satan praises the one among his devils who has caused not merely external destruction but who inflicted damage in the sphere of the human soul. Man's physical fall will be a sure consequence of his spiritual corruption. Similarly, Lucifer endeavors to break Adam's spirit through a vision of utter hopelessness.

Lessing's use of a dream in which Faust's seduction and fall take place seems the most direct correspondence between the two dramas, as Adam, too, is led through a series of dream visions while his body is left behind. However, this motif can also be found in legends, fairy tales, and in other works of literature. Parallels exist, for example, in the confessions of Saint Cyprian, in Calderón, Voltaire, and Grillparzer.

There are, however, some important differences between the concepts of Lessing and Madách. Lessing's fragments do not furnish much information about what exactly happens while Faust is asleep, but obviously his sins are committed in his dream. In Madách's play Adam's fall and expulsion from Eden and his desperate decision to kill himself occur outside the dream sphere. Madách is more consistent: the dream visions can lead into despair, but only the awakened Adam proceeds to action from there.[11]

Faust and Adam seem to react similarly to their dreams. Faust "is awakening when the devils, ashamed and angry, have already left. He thanks Providence for the warning that it intended to give him through such an instructive dream.—Now he stands more firmly in truth and virtue than ever before."[12] Adam says: "Much I have learned of all my dreams and visions./ And now I'm free to choose another way" (290). But instead of standing "more firmly in truth and virtue than ever before," he displays complete hopelessness and deepest gloom as the result of what he has seen. Only Eve's pregnancy gives him the strength to stand up to Lucifer. And it is not before that moment that the Lord appears again. Lessing's protagonist is spared these inner struggles. What Eliza Marian Butler wrote about Marlowe's Faust as compared with that of Lessing could apply to Madách's drama, too: "Marlowe's hero was spiritually destroyed, it is true, whereas Lessing's merely had a bad dream."[13]

Lessing may have decided not to complete his play because he could not resolve the conflict between the concept of human inquisitiveness as the "most noble of all drives" and the renunciation of that drive by the awakened Faust. Years later, he wrote: "If God held hidden in his right hand all truth, and in his left hand the one and only always active urge to find the truth, albeit with the provision that I would err again and again, and he told me: Choose! I would reach for his left hand with humility, saying: Give to me, Father! the full truth is for you alone!" [14] This is where Adam stands at the end of Madách's play when the Lord refuses to comment on Lucifer's visions of the future. Adam's willingness to obey God's final admonition in spite of all he has seen exemplifies Tertullian's statement, "Credo quia absurdum" (I believe as it is unreasonable). And that Latin phrase appears immediately preceding a reference to Lessing's *Fragments of an Unnamed Person* ("Wolfenbüttel'sche Fragmente") in Madách's notes as reproduced in Halász's edition. [15]

II   *The "Transformation of a Poem"*

While the parallels in the works of Lessing and Madách may be due to similarities in themes and in the authors' views, there can be no question about the very direct impact of Goethe's *Faust* on *Az ember tragédiája*. Confident of the basic originality of his own work, the Hungarian playwright made no attempt to disguise the fact that the German drama had served as his model in several ways. Goethe would probably have approved of his borrowings. What he wrote about Byron's *Manfred* could apply directly to Madách's tragedy as well:

This strange, gifted poet has absorbed my "Faust," and has taken from it the strangest food for his melancholy. He has used every theme in his own way, so that none remains what it was; and for this very reason I cannot admire him highly enough. His transformation of my poem is so much of a piece, one could give extremely interesting lectures on its likeness and unlikeness to the original. I don't deny, however, that the gloomy fire of his pervading and endless despair grows irritating in the end. And yet one's annoyance is never without admiration and respect. [16]

Madách's expository scene was clearly patterned after Goethe's "Prologue in Heaven." Of course, the poet also knew the biblical source that inspired Goethe, the confrontation between God and Satan in the Book of Job. But the influence of Goethe's dramatic scene is obvious. In both plays the archangels praise the Lord whose power and glory are evident in the creation of the universe. God, however, seems more interested in the reaction of his adversary than in the adulation of the angelic host. Mephistopheles and Lucifer have only criticism to offer and ridicule in particular the Lord's crowning achievement, the creation of man. Both plan to lead man away from God, just as Satan did in the Book of Job. But the outcome is already determined. Mephistopheles is told: "And stand ashamed when you must own perforce:/ A worthy soul through the dark urge within it / Is well aware of the appointed course." [17] Similarly, Lucifer's lack of success is predicted before he has even started his attempt: "Be tortured ever by the haunting thought / That vainly thou wilt shake thy dusty chains,/ Against thy Lord, thou shalt be impotent!" (24).

The apt self-description Lucifer uses repeatedly in this scene echoes the introduction Mephistopheles gives of himself as "the spirit which eternally denies." [18] Lucifer claims that the creation was possible only because of the eternal gap that set up a barrier to God's productive efforts and thus spurred him on: "The name that barrier bore was Lucifer,/ The Spirit that eternally denies" (23). When the Lord grants him possession of the two trees in Eden, Lucifer is confident: "A corner's all I need,/ Enough to afford a foothold for Negation,/ Whereon to raise what will destroy Thy world!" (24–25).

In both dramas man then embarks in the company of this negative spirit on his long journey through various realms of human experience. Faust, alone at night in his study, voices the same dissatisfaction with scientific endeavors as Kepler in the Prague scene. But sensual delights are not enough either: Faust is disgusted with the revelry in Auerbach's Tavern and later breaks away from the spell of the Walpurgis Night. Likewise, Sergiolus wants to be taken from the pleasures and luxuries of Rome to a more meaningful future. The two protagonists also cannot find fulfillment in the experience of absolute power. In this respect, Adam as Pharaoh parallels the aging Faust at the end of Goethe's tragedy.

Near the conclusion of either play the spirit of negation believes to have won. Again the correspondence is almost literal although the underlying meanings are not identical. After Faust has died, the chorus of Lemures exclaims, "It is all over," to which Mephistopheles replies: "Over! Stupid name./ Why over?/ All over and pure nothing—just the same!" [19] Adam thinks that by committing suicide he can end the history of mankind before it begins. That way, he will be able to say: "The comedy is ended!" Lucifer's response is: "Ah,

how absurd! The end! Vain talk! Is not / Each moment a beginning
and an ending?" (292–93). But the efforts of the negative force are
ultimately frustrated. Both plays eventually return to the extrahuman
frame, with Goethe substituting the "Mater Gloriosa" for the Lord of
the Prologue.

Throughout Madách's tragedy numerous details give evidence of
his familiarity with *Faust*. But in almost every case, a closer look
shows how the Hungarian poet used what he had found "in his own
way." Earlier works had Faust invoke the Devil, but Goethe substituted a scene in which Faust succeeds in conjuring up the Earth
Spirit. The specific meaning of this phenomenon and the implied relationship with Mephistopheles have been topics of much discussion.
Madách's use of what appears to be the same apparition seems a clear
case of borrowing. But, significantly, it is Lucifer, not Adam, who in-
vokes the Spirit and who—like Faust—must admit that he has no real
power over the forces of nature. Given the function of Madách's
Earth Spirit as a vehicle for the discussion of religious and philosophical concerns, Voinovich is overstating the case when calling the phenomenon "a clear copy" of Goethe's apparition.[20] Similarly, the related motif of the attempted creation of life in a test tube only
superficially resembles the Homunculus episode in *Faust*.

The second Prague scene is frequently singled out as an obvious
example of Goethe's influence. Károly Szász, one of the earliest reviewers, said that Kepler's dialogue with his young visitor reads like a
mere translation of Mephistopheles' conversation with the student.[21]
But here, too, the parallels are rather on the surface. Adam's advice
reflects his frustration with the limited insights of science. His attitude is similar to that of Faust's first great monologue complaining
about the futility of all his learning, and of Faust's embarrassment as
the peasants express their gratitude: "Now people's cheers to me ring
jeering fun." [22] Adam reacts the same way when reminded of his
"wisdom" that his students are anxious to share: "Ah, do not make a
mock of my poor wisdom!/ At times I blush, when people praise it
so!" (185). Both measure their knowledge by the multitude of un-
solved questions. But their basic positions are not identical. Faust is
convinced that he knows more than "those impostors, those parsons
and scribes, doctors and masters" and is not plagued by doubts. He is
sure that science will never be able to solve the final mysteries and
reveal "the inmost force that bonds the very universe." [23] Adam, on
the other hand, believes that someday man's mind will transcend its
present limitations. He is bothered by the fact that he is denied such

future knowledge. He shares with Faust the recognition of the dangers inherent in one-sided scientific striving that loses all contact with life. It is this awareness that makes him tell the young scholar:

> Take, then, these old and rotting yellow parchments,
> These mouldy folios, overlaid with dust,
> And throw them in the fire. For they prevent us
> From standing, as we should, on our own feet,
> And only spare us the fatigue of thinking.
> They bring the errors of times past and dead,
> As superstitions, into our new age. (192)

It would be a grave misinterpretation to see this as the renunciation of all search and quest. Consequently, the almost identical advice to the two students carries radically different meanings. Mephistopheles, in the guise of Faust, concludes his discourse on the academic disciplines with the statement, "Gray, dear young fellow, is all theorizing,/ And green, life's golden tree." [24] This seems to echo in Kepler's words:

> Dost thou believe thy life will last so long
> That, till thy death, thou'dst study theories?
> Let us both bid a last good-bye to school!
> Thou, with thy rosy youth, go forth and sing,
> Bask in the happy sunshine and be gay! (193)

But Mephistopheles' advice was ironic and designed to destroy all thirst for knowledge in the young man. In Madách's drama, however, Adam urges the student very seriously not to allow theories to obscure his vision of life itself.

This dissimilarity extends to the students as well. Goethe's aspiring young scholar wants "to get a power of learning" but does not like to give up "time-off and relaxation . . . like when it's summer and vacation." [25] In contrast, his counterpart in the Hungarian play is a true searcher for knowledge:

> I'm athrill with longing
> To get at least a glimpse of Nature's workshop—
> To fathom all, that all I may enjoy.
> And feel that I have earned the might to rule
> Over the worlds of Matter and of Mind! (186–87)

This desire is much closer to the attitudes of Faust and Adam than to that of the academic philistine seeking guidance from Mephistopheles.

Similar reinterpretations or changes in substance may be found in the other scenes that are reminiscent of *Faust*. Certainly Goethe's collective portrait of German small-town bourgeoisie in "Outside the City Gate" influenced Madách's depiction of nineteenth-century London. In both cases the drama's protagonist and his companion watch a colorful crowd milling about. Both authors focus on groups, not on clearly outlined individuals: each speaker represents a certain social class or occupation. Everybody enjoying a leisurely stroll on a sunny Easter afternoon in Goethe's play seems to reappear on the fairgrounds "between the Tower and the Thames" in Madách's longer and more elaborate scene. There are journeymen and students anxious to savor a few hours of pleasure. Soldiers mingle with solid burghers who complain about the state of affairs in their community. Middle-class girls cast about for the right suitor. Beggars appeal to the sympathy of passers-by, and the Gypsy woman who serves as a go-between for Adam and the girl he fancies is a reincarnation of the old witch in Goethe's scene. People are dancing and drinking, and both playwrights conclude in a more philosophical vein as evening settles in.

Yet these similarities are deceptive. Not only does Madách introduce many additional characters in his scene, but even those that appear inspired by *Faust* assume a different function. The microcosm assembled by Goethe is a mirror of the "small world" that Mephistopheles promises to show Faust, the world of the middle class of a medieval German university town. Several of the persons appearing here forecast future encounters of Faust in the first part of the tragedy. In contrast, the numerous figures Madách presents have little connection with the structure of the drama as a whole, but their function in this particular scene is quite distinct. Only the puppet show featuring the fall of man in a burlesque fashion, and the quack trying to sell the Pharaohs' elixir, Tancred's love potion, or Kepler's "Astrology," refer to earlier episodes in the play. And instead of Goethe's stance of an amused chronicler of the common weaknesses of average people, we get the view of a social critic who substitutes satire for humor.

Just as he had used the Egypt of the Pharaohs to exemplify absolute individual power, Madách selected the symbolic setting of London to depict early capitalism in its most brutal and dehumanizing form.

Money and economic power are the only recognized values; traditional human qualities no longer count. Only the students seem similar to their counterparts in *Faust*, and Adam finds them a "gladd'ning sight in this depressing world" and "the germ of better times" (216). Significantly, they are trying to escape from the "greedy business ways" of the city (215). Lucifer quickly dampens Adam's optimism, however, by pointing to two manufacturers as living examples of what this "germ of better times" will eventually become. The businessmen discuss ways of undercutting their competition by exploiting their workers. Workmen bemoan the deterioration of their conditions as the result of the introduction of machines and complain about the inhumanity of the rich. Alcohol becomes their only means of escape. If someone from the labor force stands up to a member of the possessing class, he is crushed, as is illustrated by the worker who is being led to his execution. The role of the military in this society is demonstrated when a soldier can with impunity snatch a young woman from a journeyman's arms.

The predominance of various merchants points to the fact that everything is for sale under this economic system. A jeweler is upset when people buy flowers from a little girl instead of his expensive merchandise. In order to live a musician has to prostitute himself by playing the music he detests. Begging has become a line of business. The quack pushing his worthless medicine belongs as much to this tableau as the prostitute plying her trade in the crowd. The difference between her and the middle-class girls is one of degree, not of substance. They, too, are looking for men capable of paying a price for their favors.

Another *Faust* motif in this scene is a part of this attempt to show the impact of a social and economic system on human behavior. Adam's encounter with Eve is clearly modeled after the street scene in which Faust introduces himself to Margaret. Goethe's hero sees the young woman on her way from confession and offers his company but is refused. He raves about her beauty and asks Mephistopheles to procure her for him. This is eventually done by means of jewelry Mephistopheles produces, and with the aid of Martha, a neighbor, as a go-between. Almost all these details can also be found in Madách. Eve, a middle-class girl, and her mother are coming from church. Adam's first impression, "What dignity! What virtuous modesty!" (211), echoes Faust's words in the identical situation, "God, what a lovely child! I swear / I've never seen the like of her. / She is so dutiful and pure." [26] Adam asks for the privilege of escorting the ladies through the crowd, and they indignantly reject his offer. But Eve returns quickly—strongly encouraged by her mother—when she assumes that the shabbily dressed Adam is in fact a rich ship owner. She suggests that he buy her a present, and as he wants to adorn her with pearls and diamonds, she feigns modesty by saying that gems are not for a maiden of her social standing—but only after mentioning that there are jewelry stores nearby. As in *Faust*, the suitor's evil companion produces the desired precious ornaments.

Eve's portrayal here may have been inspired by Margaret's reaction as she finds the jewel box in her cabinet: "For gold contend,/ On gold depend / All things and man . . . Poor us!" [27] Margaret, like Eve, enjoys the thought of displaying her beautiful gifts to the envy of her friends. But the fact that Eve sees an execution as the appropriate opportunity to show off her jewels indicates a shallowness of character that renders Adam's earlier words of admiration ironic. What in Margaret was a natural desire to look attractive becomes a gesture of victory in the atmosphere of keen competition of this scene. The role of Eve's mother, who had earlier advised her to keep her options open and not discourage any wealthy admirer, and Eve's willingness to go along with the stranger and throw away the gift she had just received from a less affluent young man illustrate how human relations have become mere business transactions. In this light, Madách's use of specific motifs from Goethe's drama appears almost as an attempt to parody the model scene by placing it into a totally inappropriate setting.

Another episode from Margaret's tragedy is reflected in the Constantinople scene. After Tancred's rescue of Isaura, they engage in a dialogue that underscores the impossibility of love and fulfillment in their situation. At the same time, Lucifer and Isaura's handmaiden converse, and Madách skillfully uses their banter as a humorous counterpoint to the serious exchange between the other two. Goethe had presented the identical situation in the scene set in Martha's garden where the first extensive dialogue between Faust and Margaret, as they are walking to and fro, is interrupted at regular intervals by snatches of the conversation between Mephistopheles and Martha. Both Lucifer and Mephistopheles evidence the same comic concern about being snared by a determined female. Mephistopheles carefully misinterprets all of Martha's hints. He has learned his lesson from their first encounter when he had thoughtlessly indicated his willingness to exchange rings with her, and her enthusiastic reaction had forced him into a hasty retreat: "I'd best be off before this gets absurd!/ She'd hold the very devil to his word." [28] Lucifer shows the same reaction when he turns to Adam: "Decide, sir knight! Thou wilt not leave thy love,/ And I'm unable to prevent my conquest!" (139). While comic transposition of the exchange between the principal dramatic characters to the level of their servants is an old motif in world literature, Madách certainly patterned this segment after the specific model.

Given all these examples of close correspondence between *Az ember tragédiája* and Goethe's *Faust*, the impact of the German drama on Madách cannot be denied. But, as the above detailed comparisons have demonstrated, it would be absurd to denounce the playwright as a mere imitator. Additional possible borrowings from *Faust* would give further evidence of the author's skillful adaptation of the material he found. More fruitful, however, might be a comparison of the basic concepts Goethe dealt with in *Faust* with those of the Hungarian Faustian play.

III *Goethe and Madách: Parallels and Contrasts*

"Striving" was one of Goethe's favorite terms. At the end of *Faust*, the angels, bearing Faust's "immortal essence," sing:

> Pure spirits' peer, from evil coil
> He was vouchsafed exemption;
> "Whoever strives in ceaseless toil,
> Him we may grant redemption."
> And when on high, transfigured love
> Has added intercession,
> The blest will throng to him above
> With welcoming compassion.[29]

Shortly before his death the poet commented on this passage: "In these lines . . . is contained the key to Faust's salvation. In Faust himself there is an activity which becomes constantly higher and purer to the end, and from above there is eternal love coming to his aid. This harmonizes perfectly with our religious views, according to which we cannot obtain heavenly bliss through our own strength alone, but with the assistance of divine grace." [30]

The two poles Goethe mentions here have been given different emphases by various critics and in various periods. Nineteenth-century optimism stressed Faust's "striving in ceaseless toil," his "activity

which becomes constantly higher and purer," and consequently interpreted Faust's salvation as self-salvation. After World War I
Spengler's pessimistic view of history and his use of the term "Faustian" contributed to a reevaluation of Faust's character. He was increasingly seen as the heroic loner, constantly seeking and erring, a
tragic figure who became the representative of twentieth-century
man in his rootlessness. From this perspective Goethe's protagonist
appears more closely akin to Madách's Adam. Faust is saved from the
hands of Satan only through God's incomprehensible grace. But this
view loses sight of the emphasis Goethe himself placed on Faust's
"striving."

Some of the ambiguity concerning Faust's salvation and the concept of "striving" may be due to the fact that Goethe's drama reflects
various periods in his life and different stages of his philosophical development, from the rebellious youth of the 1770s to the sage of 1831
who thought that everybody becomes a mystic in old age. Given the
much shorter time in which Madách completed his tragedy, one
would expect a more consistent and unambiguous position. But, surprisingly, it poses several of the same problems of interpretation that
are vexing *Faust* scholars.

Faust, as Goethe conceived him in his earliest draft, was a youthful
rebel who demanded the right to disregard all limitations. He is not
only reaching for higher knowledge but also wants to savor life at its
fullest. Yet he already feels that he is rushing to his own doom and
that Margaret will be swept down with him. In the fragment published in 1790, Faust is already aware of his fate when he contracts
the agreement with Mephistopheles in a newly created scene. Here
Goethe elaborates on the concept of "striving":

> And what to all mankind is apportioned
> I mean to savor in my own self's core,
> Grasp with my mind both highest and most low,
> Weigh down my spirit with their weal and woe,
> And thus my selfhood to their own distend,
> And be, as they are, shattered in the end.[31]

For the first time Faust appears here as the representative of mankind, a role which Madách's hero has throughout the play.

The tragic gap between Faust's titanic striving and his human inadequacy of the earlier version is still obvious in the completed
drama, and we find it in *Az ember tragédiája* as well: Adam fails again
and again, not only because of the shortcomings of his surroundings,

but also because of his own weakness. This human inadequacy is demonstrated in Faust when he is rebuffed by the Spirit of the Earth to whom he feels so close: "Close to the wraith you comprehend,/ Not me!" [32]

In the 1790 version Mephistopheles tries to accomplish his goals by transforming Faust's longing for the unattainable into sensual desire and sheer insatiability. But when Goethe took up work on his drama again in the early 1800s, the function of Faust's "striving"—and the role of Mephistopheles—had changed significantly. The egocentric Storm and Stress youth is now placed in a metaphysical framework, and his striving becomes a positive force. The Lord states that "man ever errs the while he strives" but unconsciously follows the right course.[33] He assigns to Mephistopheles the same role that Lucifer is given at the end of Madách's drama:

> Man all too easily grows lax and mellow,
> He soon elects repose at any price;
> And so I like to pair him with a fellow
> To play the deuce, to stir, and to entice.[34]

The double meaning of "striving" as a positive and a negative force is the basis for Faust's wager with Mephistopheles. Should he ever tire of striving and want to relax, his soul will be lost. At the end of the play Faust indeed wishes for time to stand still, but it is at the vision of the future, of millions of free people working on the soil that his efforts created. Mephistopheles has formally won his wager, but in reality this is Faust's moment of most intense activity. Striving as a positive force—to which Mephistopheles had unwittingly contributed—makes him worthy of salvation but does not automatically assure it. Yet this is the same Faust who was led by his negative striving into the very depth of depravity.

In Adam's case, the different aspects of Faust's "striving" appear distributed over separate scenes to coincide with the appropriate historic roles. But the young Adam, even while still enjoying the pleasures of Eden, displays some of the restlessness and rebelliousness of Goethe's first Faust concept. While Eve is grateful for the gift of existence, Adam's initial words pertain to power: "And to be masters over ev'rything!" His desire for freedom is already noticeable when he turns to Eve: "Dependency, I see, inspires thy being" (26). Even the expulsion from Paradise cannot diminish his pride; he feels that he can rely on his own strength to build his new world.

Faust had rejected with fierce pride any thought of the hereafter: "Beyond to me makes little matter;/ If once this earthly world you shatter,/ The next may rise when this has passed." [35] But when Adam as Danton voices the same thought, it is tinged with resignation: "I have no faith in life beyond the grave./ And, hopeless now, I fight against my Fate!" (176).

Like Faust, Adam wants to behold the active force in nature, but he knows that he is subject to it, not its master:

> Let me, then, see it as it does its work—
> A momentary glance, my soul is strong.
> I long to know how it could influence
> One, like myself, who am an entity! (44)

As Kepler, he echoes this sentiment, but we sense again his resignation. He wants to liberate himself from the fetters of human insufficiency by glancing at the spectacle of cosmic harmony, just as Faust did when viewing the sign of macrocosm:

> Ah, open to me wide, ye boundless skies,
> Your holy and mysterious Book, I pray!
> If I could only penetrate your secrets,
> I should forget the times and all around me. (161)

In the space scene Adam comes perhaps closest to the rebellious spirit of Goethe's original hero. But his defiance is the result of deepest desperation when he shouts at the Earth Spirit: "Yet I defy thee! And I fear thee not. . . . Thou canst not shake my soul. It still aspires!" (270–72). Yet he does return to earth soon after.

At the end of his life Faust is sure of having created something of lasting importance: "My path on earth, the trace I leave within it / Eons untold cannot impair." [36] In the similar words of Adam as Pharaoh, his titanic pride vis-à-vis God is emphasized: his achievement is his proof of his own strength:

> But with that monument which rises yonder,
> Methinks I may at last have found the way
> That leads to endless and enduring greatness.
> Its art will force ev'n nature to admire
> And through the ages will proclaim my fame.
> No earthquake, no disaster could destroy it—
> 'Twill show where Man was mightier than God. (55)

Yet he cannot find satisfaction in that thought. As Faust envisioned the future of what he had created, "Such teeming would I see upon this land,/ On acres free among free people stand," [37] Adam sees a new task: "Yes, for those millions I'll gain prevalence / In a free state—there is no other issue" (70). Lucifer knows, however, that this vision is an illusion just as Mephistopheles knows that the sound of spades, so delightful to the blinded Faust, does not indicate the preparation of a better future but rather the digging of his grave.

When Adam recognizes in Athens that this ideal "free state" cannot be realized, he gives up all positive striving and demands mere sensual enjoyment:

> Why should any soul
> Aspire and burn away to reach the heights?
> 'Tis wiser to strive only for one's self,
> And fill one's little span of life with bliss,
> Until we stagger, drunkenly, to Hades! (91)

But the end of the Roman scene shows that the Faustian urge is still alive in him: "Methinks my soul is set on nobler treasure / Than luxury and ease and idle pleasure" (113).

Thus, Adam, too, is spurred on by Faust's "striving" in its positive and negative form. The two heroes are akin without one being a copy of the other. Both share the feeling of being torn apart within their souls, as Faust expresses it:

> Two souls, alas, are dwelling in my breast,
> And either would be severed from its brother;
> The one holds fast with joyous earthy lust
> Onto the world of man with organs clinging;
> The other soars impassioned from the dust,
> To realms of lofty forebears winging.[38]

The words of the Lord of the "Prologue in Heaven" seem to echo in the reference to the "realms of lofty forebears." Striving becomes here the Romantic longing for one's—only vaguely perceived—original home. Adam, flying through space, senses the same inner conflict:

> And in my breast two feelings are at war.
> I feel the piteousness of Earth . . . I know
> It cramps my soaring soul, and long for freedom.
> But then nostalgic pain takes hold of me. (268)

There is an element in Adam that cannot be found in Faust. His feeling of resignation, of *Weltschmerz*, may be part of the impact Byron had on Madách, just as the portrayal of the evil companion of his striving hero may have been affected by Byron's heroes. Even more, however, Madách's attitude reflects a different poetic temperament and different life experiences.

The similarities and dissimilarities between Lucifer and Mephistopheles deserve some examination. Both are introduced in a parallel way as they criticize rather than adore the Lord. Their sarcastic comments are identical. Mephistopheles calls man "Earth's little god" who is "as weird as on the primal day" and who might be living somewhat better without the Lord's gift of "a glitter" of "Heaven's light." [39] Lucifer concurs: "Thou hast let Man into Thy mighty kitchen,/ And viewest him indulgently the while / He bungles and imagines he is God" (21).

But this first scene early establishes some very important differences. In Goethe's *Faust*, the ultimately positive function of Mephistopheles is clearly enunciated by the Lord. In Madách's drama, Lucifer is assigned the identical function only in the final scene. The initial confrontation in heaven gives no indication of his being anything but a rebellious angel. Whereas Goethe's Lord can state, "Of all the spirits of negation / The rogue has been least onerous to my mind," [40] his counterpart in Madách's drama is far from this amused tolerance. Many critics who have treated the first scene of *Az ember tragédiája* as a Goethe imitation have overlooked the significance of Madách's choice of Lucifer as God's opponent. He is the angel who had been closest to the Lord—both according to legend and to a reference in the play itself [41]—in the act of renouncing his allegiance. The stage directions specifically refer to the four archangels. After Gabriel, Michael, and Raphael have spoken up in praise of God, Lucifer is expected to make a similar statement. The pause that follows and the subsequent sharp denunciation of God's creation constitute Lucifer's sedition, and thus his relationship with the Lord is very different from that depicted in *Faust*. Consequently, Lucifer is more consistent in the execution of his plan to lead man astray. Much more is at stake for him than a wager.

Lucifer wants to use his foothold—the two trees in Eden—to make man the center of his anti-world. He intends to extinguish the Faustian drive in Adam and to bring him to a renunciation of his ties with God. He leads him to the trees of knowledge and of life and specifically gives him a ray of hope which will lead him from one era into the next:

> But when ye see how foolish the intent,
> How grievous is the conflict to be fought,
> Lest ye be overwhelmed in grey despair,
> And leave the battle, smitten to the heart,
> I give to you one little shining ray,
> To comfort you, that all things which ye saw
> Were but illusion. Lo, this ray is hope.[42]

This present makes sense only if one assumes that Lucifer's original goal is not the destruction of man but rather the creation of a godless humanity. If all human striving, motivated by hope, leads to nothing, if the senselessness of the world into which he has been thrown becomes increasingly clear to Adam, he will accept that as an indictment of God as the creator of this senselessness. Only after Lucifer realizes that his gift of hope has accomplished the opposite—despite all disappointments, man continues to search—does he change his plans and try to drive Adam to self-destruction.

Lucifer's rebellion and Adam's fall have little in common. Lucifer opposes God from his own impulse and is confident of his own strength. He constitutes the original negative force. Adam is a victim of Lucifer's seduction. The driving force in him is not Lucifer's total nihilism but rather a basically positive criticism, looking for something new and better to replace present conditions. He is constructive; his companion is destructive. The divine spark in Adam makes him worthy of salvation; Lucifer's renunciation of God, on the other hand, is final. While in other poets the fallen angel is tormented by remorse and longs for the heaven he lost, Madách's Lucifer shows no trace of such sentiment. He is quite different from the devils portrayed by Dante, Marlowe, and Milton. The concept of the salvation of the devil that Klopstock and Vigny presented in their works would not make any sense for Madách's Lucifer.

Lucifer and Mephistopheles share the goal of leading man away from God, but there is an important difference in the execution of their plans. In line with the Faust tradition Goethe's hero gives himself completely over to the devil. He agrees to the traditional conditions: Mephistopheles is to serve him in this world, and he will be the devil's servant in the next. Adam, on the other hand, only accepts Lucifer's company, not his service, in order to see the future. A minor inconsistency can be found in the London scene, obviously inspired by the parallel situation in *Faust*. Adam turns to his companion with a specific request: "But what has happened to that lovely maid?/ Come, Lucifer. Now prove thy potency,/ By helping me to win her ear" (218). And Lucifer produces the desired jewelry just as Mephistopheles had done.

In this scene Madách emphasizes in his portrayal of Lucifer some of the traditional features of the devil: the money given to the Gypsy becomes quicksilver, the jewelry turns into snakes—just as the wine Mephistopheles produced in Auerbach's Tavern changed into flames. Lucifer mocks the Gypsy's false claims of her closeness to Satan when she neither recognizes nor relishes his devilish handshake. And the description Eve's mother gives of him brings to mind the image of the devil as established through the centuries: "I've no objection even to his friend./ Despite his hook nose and his bandy legs,/ He seems a decent man, well on in years" (224). Some of the features shared by Lucifer and Mephistopheles are certainly due to the fact that both authors utilized characteristics of the traditional devil. Mephistopheles, however, frequently ridicules this "devilish" image of his and implies that it is just one of his disguises. The humor of the "rogue," which makes him tolerable even to the Lord and which frequently leads to self-mockery, is alien to Lucifer who is rather two-dimensional in comparison. He stays within his role throughout the play and offers sarcasm instead of humor.

It would be too narrow an interpretation to see in Lucifer just the Devil of the Judeo-Christian tradition, even though he emphasizes that role on occasion. Attempts have been made to view him as the representative of matter—counterbalancing Adam, the representative of the idea—or as cold intellect—furnishing the contrast to the emotions of Adam and Eve. Yet neither interpretation will hold up under closer scrutiny. Gabriel praises the Lord for having filled the boundless space with matter, and Lucifer himself credits God with having created matter. In his plans Lucifer can use matter—and Adam's material striving—but this is not his exclusive realm. Yet he is not the embodiment of cool rationality either, despite his words when he observes Adam and Eve:

> Why do I listen to their tender wooing?
> I'll turn away, lest I should have to blush
> As cold and calculating intellect
> Grew envious of their weak and childish minds? (29)

This very statement shows that he is not just "cold and calculating intellect" since he is concerned about becoming touched by something emotional. And his rebellion against God springs more from emotion than from rational thinking.

A similar ambiguity can be found in Goethe's Mephistopheles as well. Perhaps the inconsistencies in the portrayals of both "devils" can be reduced if their self-characterization as the "spirit of negation" is taken at its basic meaning. Both represent absolute negativity, nihilism, chaos. Faust seems to recognize that when he calls Mephistopheles at their first meeting "hoar Chaos's fantastic son." [43] In this sense, then, Madách does not simply "translate" Goethe's term into Hungarian as Voinovich claims.[44] On the most profound level Lucifer and Mephistopheles are alike. Both are opposed to anything positive or creative, be it in the realm of matter or spirit. Therefore, they are equally capable of switching roles with the dramas' protagonists. Either will frequently make ironic comments that rectify distortions caused by Adam's or Faust's idealism or naiveté. In this way, both are often necessary complements to the heroes, and their criticism is aimed at real shortcomings and problems. Of course, neither of them is interested in improving those conditions but rather in ridiculing human weakness and in demonstrating that nothing that exists is of any value.

But in pointing out problem areas or deplorable situations, both also frequently become spokesmen for the views of the two playwrights. This has contributed to the difficulties in deciding whether Lucifer's presentation of history is in the main factual or constitutes gross distortion. Goethe once commented on the opinion of Jean-Jacques Ampère: "Concerning Faust, his remarks are . . . clever, since he not only notes, as part of myself, the gloomy, discontented striving of the principal character, but also the scorn and bitter irony of Mephistophiles." [45] This view is equally applicable to Madách and the two opposing and yet complementary characters he created. Faust's "two souls" have been assigned to two separate beings, as it were.

Faust and Adam share the inability to refute their companions' ironic comments when their positions are challenged as being based on illusions. Adam's anguished "Enough, enough, thou everlasting sophist!" (196) is an almost verbatim repetition of Faust's answer to Mephistopheles in a similar situation. And just as Mephistopheles occasionally unmasks Faust's pretended lofty aspirations as animalistic impulses, Lucifer mockingly reacts to Adam's enthusiasm at the sight

of Eve in the London scene: "She's surely not a novelty to thee?"
(209). This is again an echo of Mephistopheles' cold but accurate
comment on Faust's despair over the destruction he has brought into
Margaret's life, "She is not the first." [46] Adam is touched as he sees
Eve coming from church, but Lucifer immediately interprets her motivation: "She went there to be seen . . . perhaps to see" (209).
Adam is shy in approaching her, and Lucifer encourages him: "Oh,
never fear, man. Thou art not a novice!/ We'll have a look at her. She
may be bought. . . ." Despite Adam's exclamation, "Be still!", Lucifer continues: "She may be dearer than the others" (211). Eve's subsequent behavior attests to the accuracy of his assessment.

Adam later reacts similarly by "laying his hands on Lucifer's lips"
and shouting, "Ah, say no more!" (285) when, in the desolation of the
ice region, Lucifer presents a relativistic panorama of human history
in which all great deeds are seen as the results of material circumstances. Yet Lucifer's relativism may also reflect Madách's insights.
He himself had experienced incidents of misunderstandings arising
from the fact that people depend on various needs and their satisfaction. The Eskimo sees Adam's emotional outburst and asks Lucifer
whether his friend's anger is due to his being hungry. Lucifer's response, "Nay, on the contrary. That's why he's in wrath!", elicits
Adam's annoyed reply, "Another sorry and untimely jest!" But Lucifer is very serious when he states:

> It is no jest, but truth. Thy reasoning
> Is that of one who's sated—thy companion's
> Is the philosophy of empty bellies.
> With arguments, ye'll ne'er convince each other.
> But ye'd agree at once if thou didst hunger,
> Or else if he could have his fill of food. (282–83)

Perhaps Pál Szontágh's often sarcastic attitude, which complemented
Madách's own nature, contributed to the depiction of Lucifer's character, just as Goethe's friend Merck had lent some of his features to
Mephistopheles. But often Lucifer speaks for Madách himself, and
occasionally this leads to a breach in the characterization of the
"devil." In the Constantinople scene Lucifer sums up the poet's observations about the relationship between the sexes:

> Thy human race is really very mad.
> Either Man sees in Woman but the means
> Of gratifying low desire, and then,

With brutal hands, he robs her tender face
Of poetry, love's chief and crowning grace,
And, by his action, doth himself despoil;
Or, like a god, he sets her on an altar,
And bleeds for her, or struggles uselessly,
While her frustrated kisses are all wasted.
Why can he never treat her as a woman,
Who, as a woman, hath her sphere and place? (140–41)

Goethe and Madách extended the destructive attitude of their "devils" beyond the realm of morality by making them the embodiment of all negation. Both evil spirits hate anything good or pure, beautiful or harmonious. They reject the Greek ideals of classical beauty in very similar terms. Lucifer's enthusiastic embracement of "the new trend they call Romanticism" (200), whose essence to him is distortion and ugliness, is again reminiscent of Mephistopheles' attitude which, incidentally, also reflects Goethe's own opposition to the "unhealthy" new literary movement. Another parallel, however, is more significant than their esthetic preferences. As the representatives of chaos and destruction, they have no power in the confrontation with the positive creative force of motherhood. Mephistopheles is unable to accompany Faust into the realm of the "Mothers" in his quest for Helen of Troy. In this connection, Goethe's use of the "Mater Gloriosa" in the symbolic final scene of *Faust* to personify God's splendor is important. What the "Chorus Mysticus" praises as "Woman Eternal," triumphant over the spirit of negation, appears as the divine mother. The fact that in *Az ember tragédiája* Lucifer's ultimate defeat comes about through Eve's motherhood establishes a more profound parallel between the two dramas than Madách's borrowing of certain minor details for his characterization of Eve.

In view of these parallels in basic concepts, and especially in view of the similar scope of thought presented in Madách's work, the term "Hungarian Faust" does not appear totally inappropriate, as long as the originality of the drama and the intellectual independence of its author are recognized. As a philosophical drama, Madách's tragedy holds a position in Hungarian literature that is quite comparable to that of *Faust* in the German world of letters.

Yet, as Jenő Bencze—among others—emphasized, in many ways the two tragedies constitute exact opposites.[47] The Hungarian scholar rejects the epithet "Hungarian Faust" as completely misleading. *Faust* is the drama of an individual and his progress. Thus it is related to the literary genre of the *Entwicklungsroman,* the novel in which the inner development of its protagonist is traced. The stress on duality throughout Goethe's work is a typical German feature for which there is no equivalent in the Hungarian drama. The character of Faust, incorporating much of Goethe's own experience, is a real and complete person, whereas Madách's Adam and Eve are abstractions operating in an abstract space.

Bencze rightly states that the very title of Madách's play says something about the spirit in which the poet conceived his drama. *Faust* is vibrant with the optimism of a man in control of his existence. The Hungarian playwright, on the other hand, had suffered much and was weakened and in poor health when he wrote *Az ember tragédiája.* He had a natural inclination toward pessimism and could look at human existence only from an angle of finality and irreparability. Like so many of his contemporaries, he was a student of Schopenhauer. But his pessimism, which gives unity to his work, is a combination of his temperament, his experiences, and his philosophical preferences. It is hard to disagree with Bencze's overall assessment: "Different in conception and structure, Madách's work is thus neither an imitation nor the pessimistic counterpart of *Faust.* It is the work of a man who has studied much and meditated much about history, just as are the great philosophical works of all literatures—*Faust* unquestionably included." [48]

While many of Bencze's points are valid, some of his arguments could be questioned. The duality expressed in *Faust* is not necessarily restricted to a German mode of thinking. Madách's Faustian hero voices the same feeling of being torn apart by the "two souls" in his breast. And Adam is not just an abstraction but a very real character as well. Of course, the constant role changes make him appear less uniform than Goethe's protagonist. With somewhat greater justification Eve could be called an "abstraction." But in that respect, she comes close to Goethe's concept of Helena in the second part of his tragedy, or to the role of Margaret in her reappearance as intercessor for her former lover in the final scene of *Faust.*

One aspect, only touched upon by Bencze, seems worth stressing. Adam is "at the same time a collective symbol and an exceptional individual." [49] It is true the *Faust* deals with universal questions and reaches beyond the realms of individual experience. Yet Goethe's drama is basically the tragedy of one outstanding individual. Madách, on the other hand, used one man to represent all of humanity. He did not select the title "Tragedy of Mankind" for his drama because he would certainly have agreed with Goethe's observation that "mankind" is an abstract term, that there have always been and always will be only individuals. But Adam, destined to become the ancestor of all men, actually represents all of them.

Madách's other dramatic attempts had focused on individuals and their fates. With the conscious decision to deal with the totality of human history, he went beyond the scope of a Faustian tragedy. Goethe's *Faust* was a product of the eighteenth and early nineteenth centuries. Its time of origin spans the period from Storm and Stress to Romanticism, and it bears the traces of the changing literary movements. *Az ember tragédiája,* written in the second half of the nineteenth century when Realism began to emerge as an important trend in European literature, is essentially an example of late Romanticism, representative of a unique literary genre for which Goethe's drama had helped lay the foundation: the *poème d'humanité*, the poem about mankind and its progress in the course of history.

CHAPTER 6

A Poem of Mankind: Madách and European Romanticism

I *The* Poème d'Humanité

T HE VALUE of influence studies is somewhat limited. Not much is accomplished by demonstrating that an author was familiar with someone else's works, and that this acquaintance left some traces behind. Yet much of Madách scholarship has focused on such investigations, probing into the writer's familiarity with Hans Christian Andersen, Ludwig Büchner, George Noël Gordon Lord Byron, Dante Alighieri, Carl Julius Weber (Demokritus), Heinrich Heine, Victor Hugo, Wilhelm Jordan, Marie Louis Alphonse Lamartine, Hughes Felicité de Lamennais, Martin Luther, John Milton, Percy Bysshe Shelley, Alexandre Soumet, Alfred de Vigny, and others.

It may be more productive to place Madách's drama into a wider framework by relating it to the European literary and philosophical landscape of the time. For Western Europe, the middle of the nineteenth century marked, as Béla Németh phrased it, "the dusk of Romanticism in the shadow of Positivism." [1] Romanticism had run its course in Germany and England, whereas France was the scene of the contest between Romantic tendencies and the newly emerging Realistic movement. Thus, the period when Madách became his country's outstanding philosophical dramatist was one of competing literary trends in Europe. Obviously this struggle existed in Hungary as well, even though West European movements materialized there after some delay, and the political events of the time left a unique imprint on her literature.

A favorite poetic genre of Romanticism, especially in France, was the *poème d'humanité,* the attempt to show in dramatic or epic form the development of mankind through one or more of its outstanding representatives. Writers thus tried to find an answer to the age-old question of man's purpose on earth. In the preface to *La Légende des siècles* (The Legend of the Centuries) Victor Hugo sums up their objectives: "To express mankind in a type of cyclic work; to paint it successively and simultaneously, in all its aspects, history, fable, philosophy, religion, science, which amount to one single and immense upward movement toward the light; to make appear in a sort of mirror, both dark and bright . . . that great figure, both unique and manifold, dismal and radiant, fatal and holy: Man." [2] Lamartine, Quinet, Vigny, and Soumet could have accepted this as a summary of their intentions. Except for the degree of optimism voiced here, this is also an apt description of *Az ember tragédiája*. Wilhelm Hoegen, one of the first to treat the *poème d'humanité* or *Menschheitsdichtung* as a distinct genre, pointed out that this idea of treating man's history in extensive poems was somehow in the air at that time.[3] The Romantic preoccupation with the individual and with universality, with history and with metaphysical questions led almost inevitably to the development of a genre whose roots may lie in medieval chronicles and epics, but even more in Dante's *Divine Comedy*, Milton's *Paradise Lost*, and Goethe's *Faust*.

A number of scholars have emphasized how well Madách's drama fits into this genre. László Juhász called Madách "a disciple of French Romanticism" and discussed in detail his familiarity with French literature. The claim, however, that Lamartine's impact on Madách equals that of Goethe seems open to question.[4] Wolfgang Margendorff counted *Az ember tragédiája* among the "great dramatic world poems" but did not proceed to any systematic discussion of the genre and of parallels in the works he listed.[5] This approach was then taken by János Barta who saw Madách's Adam as the last of the Faustian rebels. While emphasizing the importance of the mythical framework for the *poème d'humanité*, Barta suggests two characteristic features to be found in this genre: through a series of dreams, apparitions, or visions, mankind's great problems are presented, usually in chronological order; and the protagonist undergoes a number of role changes during the work. Barta rightly views Madách's drama not as an imitation of French *poèmes d'humanité* but rather as the realization of their potentialities.[6] Sőtér and Károly Horváth have shown additional European parallels.[7]

Enikő Basa gives the most thorough treatment of Madách's work and the *poème d'humanité*.[8] In addition to a concise summary of the pertinent research, she deals in detail with the relevant poems of Shelley, Byron, Lamartine, and Hugo. Of special importance is her discussion of Dante's, Milton's, and Goethe's influences on the genre.

After going into the similarities in Byron's *Cain* and *Manfred,*
Shelley's *Prometheus Unbound,* Lamartine's *La Chute d'un ange,*
Hugo's *La Légende des siècles,* and Madách's *Az ember tragédiája,*
Basa concludes: "The affinity is due partly to the debt owed by all of
these poems to *Paradise Lost* and *Faust* in both form and theme. Yet,
the analogies are not extensive for each poet follows his own beliefs
and chooses his own style of expression." [9]

Despite Goethe's vocal rejection of what he considered "Romantic," his works, especially *Faust,* represent the single most powerful
influence on nineteenth-century Romanticism and on the *poème
d'humanité.* In the case of Byron—in spite of his denials—this is particularly obvious. His Manfred is a Faustian hero who is isolated from
society and surrounded by people incapable of comprehending his
drive. But in Byron's work this isolation is part of a feeling of despair
rarely to be found in Goethe. Byron's drama ends with Manfred's
death, Goethe's with Faust's salvation. *Cain* also presents the Faustian loner, but through the use of a biblical myth the universality of his
rebellion is stressed more than in the individual tragedy of *Manfred,*
and the metaphysical setting brings his fate closer to that of Madách's
Adam. Lucifer's role in *Cain* is similar to those of the spirits of negation in Goethe and Madách. Like Madách's Lucifer, he tries to mislead man through visions of other ages. But the end has neither the
force of "Woman Eternal" nor God's encouragement to struggle on
in confidence. Byron's fragment *The Deformed Transformed* also
shows Goethe's impact and features the role changes that Barta saw
as a criterion of the *poème d'humanité.* And, as in Madách's play, the
protagonist embarks on his journey to adventure in the company of
the devil.

Shelley's optimism provides a striking contrast to Byron's attitude.
The message of *Queen Mab* is that reason and morality will eventually prevail, and mankind's development is toward a more perfect
state. Again a series of visions, albeit not very clearly outlined, traces
the past, present, and future history of humanity. As in Byron, traditional religion is viewed as a means of enslaving man and is rejected;
unlike Byron, Shelley believes in the healing power of nature. *Prometheus Unbound* continues Shelley's discussion of his unorthodox
religious views. Milton's rebellious Satan experiences a reincarnation
here, struggling against a tyrannical God. But Shelley's use of classical rather than Christian mythology makes this relationship appear
less offensive. Prometheus, too, is shown the future and recognizes
the senselessness of the sacrifice of Christ and the inability of the hu-

man race to find freedom through revolution. Man can reach perfection within himself and by himself. Only if the individual overcomes hate and embraces love can he be free.

In French Romanticism many of these themes and trends are brought together. True to the spirit of the period, however, much of its literary production has remained fragmentary. Alfred de Vigny offered a panorama of human history in his *Poèmes antiques et modernes*, but the arrangement of individual poems is somewhat accidental and does not amount to a cyclic overview. Yet we do find the Faustian individual in his *Moses* who, according to the author, represents merely a mask for the man of genius of all centuries. *Éloa* presents the Miltonic theme of Satan's fall and an attempt to save the fallen angel through love, a theme that recurs in numerous variants during this period. The role of the female, as suggested in "La Maison du Berger" (The Shepherd's Home) with its famous question, "Eva, qui donc es-tu?" ("Eve, who are you after all?"), echoes Goethe's "Woman Eternal" and points forward to Madách's Eve.[10]

Alexandre Soumet's *La divine épopée ou l'enfer racheté* (The Divine Epic, or Hell Redeemed) belongs in the list of *poèmes d'humanité* despite its doubtful literary merits. Edgar Quinet dealt with the Faustian individual in his *Prométhé* (Prometheus). *Ahasvérus*, his prose poem about the Wandering Jew, features once again the series of historic visions: God, dissatisfied with his creation, selects four historic periods to show his angels the world's corruption. The motif of continuous role changes—up to the final salvation through love and faith—recurs here also.

Lamartine's goal was more ambitious. He wanted to portray the destiny of the human race in an epic poem of gigantic proportions. His preface to *La Chute d'un ange* (The Fall of an Angel) asks: "The human soul and the successive phases through which God fulfills its perfectible destiny, is that not the most beautiful theme of poetic songs?" [11] And the preface to *Jocelyn* states that the time for the individual heroic poem is over; the task of perfecting man is a collective and eternal mission; humanity is the poet's subject: "But with this subject so vast that each poet, each century perhaps, can write only a single page of it, it became necessary to find for it its form, its drama, its individual types." [12] The epic of which *La Chute d'un ange* and *Jocelyn* represent the first and last parts has remained a fragment. Cédar, expelled from the ranks of the angels because of his love for the mortal Daïdha, may gradually return to his position through a succession of ordeals. In *Jocelyn* the nine reincarnations appear completed, and Cédar-Jocelyn and his beloved Daïdha-Laurence can be reunited for eternity. Unfortunately, Lamartine's characters are passive and rather colorless. It is hard to see how they contribute to the perfection of mankind. As in Shelley, we encounter symbols and abstractions or personifications, not creatures of flesh and blood.

If Lamartine had completed his other epic of humanity, *Les Visions*, there might be the French equivalent of Madách's drama, at least in concept if not in artistic quality. But we have only the outline for the ten historic visions, and some fragments of the first and eighth visions. Éloïm, Lamartine's hero, is led by the spirit of God through various periods, including the time of the Old Testament, classical antiquity, the age of Jesus, the beginning of chivalry, and the French Revolution, to the end of the world and the onset of eternity. As in *Az ember tragédiája*, the protagonist's female counterpart appears in a number of scenes, representing positive and negative aspects of womanhood.

The emphasis Lamartine placed on history is also characteristic of the work usually considered the greatest *poème d'humanité* in French literature, Victor Hugo's *La Légende des siècles*, whose remarkable parallels with Madách's drama will be discussed separately.

While the tendencies outlined here are most obvious in France, they can be seen in other literatures of nineteenth-century Europe, too. Madách's deliberate universality sets his work apart from a play like Adam Mickiewicz's *Dziady* (Forefather's Day) which is more a "poem of Poland" than a "poem of humanity." But the Polish work shares many of the features discussed above. George Sand, who judged it superior to Goethe's *Faust* and Byron's *Manfred* because of its more exact balance between dream and reality, emphasized that Mickiewicz's hero Konrad is a representative of modern man. His cry sounds like the voice of all humanity protesting against the reign of evil and imploring divine intercession for mankind.[13] Allardyce Nicoll sees another Polish work, Zygmunt Krasinski's *Nieboska Komedja* (The Undivine Comedy), as the equivalent of Madách's drama.[14] Its gloomy vision of the social struggle between the aristocracy and the masses, leading Europe into chaos, could have been produced by Madách's Lucifer. But Krasinski has Christ triumphant at the end, just as Madách, twenty-five years later, would have the victorious Lord reappear. Krasinski's *Irydion*—despite its nationalistic emphasis—seems related to the Romantic *poème d'humanité* and features its metaphysical framework.

The early works of Henrik Ibsen are characterized by the competing forces of Romanticism and Realism. *Peer Gynt* is not completely
outside the tradition of the *poème d'humanité.* Its message is meant
for all people. As in *Faust* and *Az ember tragédiája,* the female sup-
plies the ultimate solution. But Ibsen's focus is somewhat narrower
than that of many of the other poets: he specifically wanted to casti-
gate the weaknesses of his Norwegian audience, and the view of history is almost completely absent.

Wagner's *Ring of the Nibelung* cycle is occasionally seen as a poem
of mankind. The German writer-composer, however, in his efforts to
create a total work of art, goes beyond the realm of literature. It
would not be justifiable to treat his oeuvre from a merely literary
point of view. But his attempt to discuss the purpose of human existence by bringing together human struggles and the world of the gods
places him, too, in the Romantic tradition.

Those nineteenth-century German works that are more representative of the genre are of debatable literary merit, but their connection with Madách's play warrants their brief mention. Maria Farnek
found some evidence for Madách's possible knowledge of Wilhelm
Jordan's *Demiurgos,* an epic that is rightly forgotten today.[15] Lucifer
leads the good spirit Agathadaemon in human form through the
world of man in order to demonstrate that only suffering can keep
humanity from boredom and stagnation. Many of the disappointments experienced by Agathadaemon-Heinrich are reminiscent of
episodes in Madách's tragedy. But apart from their somewhat similar
interpretations of the function of evil, which had become commonplace since Goethe anyway, the philosophies of the two poets have
little in common.

Adolf von Wilbrandt's drama *Der Meister von Palmyra* (The Master of Palmyra) combines the Ahasvérus motif with the concept of
transmigration of souls. Apelles, the Master of Palmyra, has been
granted his wish for immortality and goes through various periods of
history as an active participant or as an observer. In each era he encounters his beloved Zoe in a different reincarnation. Finally he desires death as he recognizes the wisdom of limiting the lifespan of
man whose immortal being can then go through various forms and
existences in order to become worthy of the reunion with God.
Wilbrandt, the director of the Vienna Burgtheater when Ede Paulay
staged the very successful first production of *Az ember tragédiája* at
the National Theater in neighboring Budapest, was probably familiar

with the play and was influenced by it. But his Apelles—much like Byron's Manfred—is a Faustian individual, not a representative of mankind.

Adolf Friedrich von Schack's epic poem *Nächte des Orients oder die Weltalter* (Oriental Nights or The World's Epochs) describes in twelve chapters the journey of its first-person narrator through visions of history. These have been conjured up by Ali, a mysterious magician whose satirical comments seem to echo Madách's Lucifer. Schack's protagonist, moving from one disappointing experience to the next, eventually realizes that the golden age lies in the future, not in the past. The final apotheosis of Bismarck's *Reich*—in obvious contrast to the atmosphere of gloom and despair at the beginning of the poem—is far from the message of the Hungarian *poème d'humanité*, and despite some parallels it is not very likely that Schack knew Madách's play.

Another German work, however, was conceived and executed as a direct response to what its author viewed as Madách's atheism and hostility toward religion. Eduard Hlatky wrote *Weltenmorgen* (Dawn of the World) from a dogmatic Catholic position. The three "actions" of his dramatic poem, "The Fall of the Angels," "The Fall of Man," and "The First Sacrifice," are only loosely connected and furthermore interrupted by three insertions, "Previous Action in God," "Heavenly Interlude," and "Prelude in Hell." Hlatky traces the events from the creation to the crime of Cain. Lucifer's rebellion springs from his unwillingness to accept humans—the Virgin Mary and God's representative on earth—as superior to him, a spiritual being. From this perspective the French Revolution and the advances made by science, hailed by French Romanticists as landmarks on the way to human perfection and to reunion with God, are portrayed as the works of the devil. Repeated references to *Az ember tragédiája* underscore the poet's intention to correct Madách's "distortions." Hlatky's almost forgotten poem lacks the dramatic tension of the Hungarian tragedy. It is burdened with theological discussions, and its characters remain pale personifications and allegories.

A survey of the development of the *poème d'humanité* in the nineteenth century shows that—quite apart from their other artistic shortcomings—the works of Schack, Wilbrandt, and Hlatky are epigonic, utilizing a genre whose time was over. Madách's drama was the ultimate and most outstanding realization of a poetic tendency of Romanticism. It is in the Hungarian play that the various strands evident in other European literatures are woven together into the fabric of one significant work. Madách's Adam is akin to Dante's visionary, led by Milton's rebellious Satan, and driven by a Faustian urge to explore and go beyond commonly accepted limitations. Like Milton's Adam and Byron's Cain, he is shown the future of mankind. Madách presents a selected number of historical miniatures reminiscent of the intentions of Lamartine and Hugo. His Eve is "Woman Eternal," despite her shortcomings, guide and redeemer of man, a role found in most of the *poèmes d'humanité*. But in none of the other works do we find the cohesiveness provided by the Hungarian author when he made Adam an active participant in the historic visions rather than a mere spectator. The intertwining of individual tragedy, philosophical view of world history, and metaphysical confrontation is not to be found elsewhere in European Romanticism.

II   Hugo and Madách: Two Romanticists Look at Human History

It is not surprising that Madách should be called a "disciple of French Romanticism." He belonged to the generation of Hungarian writers after 1830 for whom revolutionary France had become the cultural ideal. Mór Jókai was later to say, "We were all Frenchmen." While German Romanticism was generally ignored in Hungary, French Romantic works were widely admired and imitated. The experience of 1848 and of the Bach regime further diminished the importance of German cultural influences.

Of the French authors of the time, Victor Hugo probably exerted the greatest impact.[16] Baron József Eötvös, who translated his *Angelo* into Hungarian, served as a major intermediary, especially through the 1837 article "Hugo Victor mint drámai költő" (Victor Hugo as a Dramatist) in which he stressed that a playwright must possess a "moral conviction" to promote justice and to instruct his audience; but in order to do that, his work must also provide pleasure.

Madách may have tried consciously to heed Eötvös's advice. He shunned dreary didacticism and tried to create a work that could entertain and stimulate critical thinking at the same time. It is an interesting coincidence that his play, which in many ways constitutes the dramatic counterpart of Hugo's *La Légende des siècles*, was drafted at the exact time when the French epic appeared in print. The first series of Hugo's *poème d'humanité* was published in the fall of 1859.[17]

Starting with Károly Szász, the Hungarian translator of *La Légende des siècles*, students of Magyar literature have on occasion compared the two works. Ignace Kont claimed that *Az ember tragédiája* might have been influenced directly by Hugo's "petites épopées" ("little epics"): "If one wants to bring out the influences that exert themselves in this dramatic poem . . . one should certainly turn one's eyes to *La Légende des siècles* rather than to *Faust.*" [18] But when the first excerpts from Hugo's work—"Le Sacre de la femme" (The Consecration of Woman) and "Le Marriage de Roland" (Roland's Marriage)—were published in the *Revue des Deux Mondes* of September 1, 1859, Madách had already been working on his play for more than six months, and some of its basic ideas had been on his mind for years. Voinovich investigated certain parallels between the two poems.[19] Juhász stated that Madách's view of women and his pantheism could in part be attributed to his contact with the oeuvre of Hugo.[20] More recently, Barta and Sőtér have included references to Hugo in their Madách studies, as have György Vajda and Mihály Szegedy-Maszák.[21] Enikö Basa devoted a large part of her thesis on the *poème d'humanité* to the two works. French literary scholarship, on the other hand, has taken little notice of Madách's poem.[22]

Madách certainly was familiar with and interested in Hugo, quoting him in his correspondence (ÖM 2, 950) and using the dedication from *Cromwell* for his own *Lantvirágok.*[23] His library contained a copy of *Ruy Blas*, and he acquired Szász's translation of the *Légende* as soon as it appeared. He probably felt akin to the French poet whose political commitment he shared—Hugo also served in parliament—and whose philosophical and religious attitudes were close to his. Both authors wrote during a period of disillusionment with the political situation, Hugo in exile on Guernsey, waiting and hoping for a change in the power structure, Madách in the seclusion of Alsósztregova after experiencing personal and national tragedy. Hungarian scholar György Mihály Vajda emphasizes this similarity: "Hugo was in actual emigration, Madách in internal emigration; they both conducted a self-examination following an abortive revolution; they both approached the immense epic subjects with the same introverted lyricism and the same dramatic tension." [24] Although both seem to report factually on historic events, personal experience also shaped their works: Hugo's bitterness toward the regime of Napoléon III emerges frequently, and certain poems stem from his spiritualist experimentation.

Some of the similarities between the two works are striking. Both show in fifteen segments the development of humanity from Eden into the distant future, and Madách could have accepted most of

Hugo's objectives as his own goals. A number of the historic periods selected by the two writers are nearly or completely identical. The state of innocence in Paradise, depicted in Madách's second scene, has its equivalent in Hugo's "D'Ève à Jésus" (From Eve to Jesus), especially in "Le Sacre de la femme" (The Consecration of Woman). The fall of Adam and Eve illustrates man's early sinfulness in Madách's play; "La Conscience" (The Conscience) has the identical function. The Roman scene of *Az ember tragédiája* shows the same moral decay as "Décadence de Rome: Au Lion d'Androclès" (Decadence of Rome: On Androcles' Lion). In "Le Cycle héroique chrétien" (The Heroic Christian Cycle) and in "Les Chevaliers errants" (The Wandering Knights) Hugo treats the medieval chivalry of Madách's Constantinople scene. Oriental despotism is dealt with in "Les Trônes d'Orient: Zim-Zizimi" (The Oriental Thrones: Zim-Zizimi) and in the portrayal of Adam as Pharaoh. Madách looks at the social problems of his own century in his London scene, Hugo in his segment "Maintenant" (Now). Even a glimpse at the future is given, both in Madách's Phalanstery and in his ice region, and in Hugo's "Vingtième Siècle" (Twentieth Century).

The two works establish the mythological framework and present initially the attitudes of God and his adversary toward creation; Hugo's "Puissance égale bonté" (Power Equals Goodness) corresponds to the first scene in the Hungarian drama. At the end of the historical panorama both return to the extrahuman powers, in "Hors des Temps: La Trompette du jugement" (Beyond the Times: The Trumpet of Judgment) in *La Légende des siècles*, and in the final confrontation between Lucifer and the Lord in *Az ember tragédiája*.

Since Hugo and Madách selected similar epochs, a number of specific parallels can be shown. In addition, the Hungarian work also features some of Hugo's favorite themes, such as the many variations of the "protector-protégé" relationship in *La Légende*, where frequently the "knight in shining armor" or the "heroic loner" comes to the aid of someone young and vulnerable.[25] Madách repeatedly offers the same motif, most clearly in Tancred's rescue of Isaura. Hugo used the same name for the orphaned "protégée" in "La Confiance du marquis Fabrice" (The Trust of Marquis Fabrice). In keeping with this relationship, Madách's Adam later repeats his chivalrous gesture, anachronistically brandishing a sword in the utopian Phalanstery.

More significant, however, are some of the philosophical similarities. Both writers held unorthodox religious views but professed a basic belief in God. Organized religion appears as a negative force, enslaving man rather than setting him free. The attitude toward the church in Madách's Constantinople scene, where heretics are led to the stake because of their opposition to *Homoousionism*, is the same that Hugo displays in "Les Raisons de Momotombo" (Momotombo's Reasons) which details the horrors of the Inquisition. The two authors look at human sinfulness, but while Madách focuses on Adam's fall, Hugo, in "La Conscience," presents Cain's slaying of Abel without really addressing the question of the origin of evil. Yet a scene like "Le Crapaud" (The Toad), in which children torture a toad to death, ties in with the traditional concept of original sin. Understandably, some of the very severe attacks on both poets have come from the Catholic Church, although Madách did not share Hugo's experience of seeing his works on the *Index of Forbidden Books*.

In their overview of history the two authors dwell on its darker aspects. In this connection, a letter of Madách to Károly Szász is quite illuminating. Szász had suggested the inclusion of a segment dealing with the Reformation. Madách replied that he had indeed considered that possibility but had decided against it because he did not know how to present that movement as also having failed (ÖM 2, 947). In both works there is continuous disillusionment but also some progress, and both writers see the human urge for liberty as a driving force. The French Revolution is therefore depicted as a very significant event. Madách deals with it directly whereas Hugo merely hints at it, even though he had stated in his preface that he would pursue the fate of the human race "from Eve, the mother of men, to the Revolution, the mother of peoples." [26] "Dix-septième Siécle: Les Mercenaires" (Seventeenth Century: The Mercenaries) pays homage to the Swiss people who fought for freedom in the past. But Hugo makes it quite clear that liberty for all mankind will not originate in their country. The "Giant Knight" in "1453" identifies himself as "France" and pledges to come back to bring liberty. The two works contain hidden or direct criticism of existing political or economic conditions, and it has been argued that some of the Saint-Simonian views of Madách's London scene were inspired by Hugo's philosophical position. [27]

With all these parallels, however, some very important formal, thematic, and philosophic differences should not be overlooked. The most obvious contrast is, of course, in the dissimilar forms of the two *poèmes d'humanité*. Madách's drama is much more uniform when compared with Hugo's collection of "petites épopées" of greatly varying length and tone. But although Hugo's poems range from the lyrical to the epic, their character is largely dramatic, and his frequent use of dialogue brings much of the work closer to Madách's play than might appear at first glance. Yet Madách's consistent use of the dramatic mode forces him to rely on a more realistic treatment of the various episodes, while Hugo's choice of epic poetry makes it easier to move to the level of symbolic or allegoric representation. Perhaps the "Satyre" (Satyr) segment is the most striking example. The transition from the realistic portrayal of mythological figures to the awe-inspiring vision of the future by the Satyr who is growing to gigantic dimensions would certainly be unthinkable in dramatic literature. On the other hand, Madách also has a number of purely symbolic episodes, such as the vision at the end of the Roman scene or the final *danse macabre* in London.

Madách's clever use of a central hero adds to the unity and coherence of his play. The French writer instead substituted thematic centrality in his effort to show that all of humanity's struggles combine to form "one single and immense upward movement toward the light." But the reader is easily led astray and becomes absorbed in the individual action without being able to see the universal trend at the same time. The *poème d'humanité* with Hugo tends toward a collection of human poems.

Two other differences spring from Madách's choice of a central figure: he focuses on the great historical personages while Hugo places equal emphasis on average people and collective bodies. Furthermore, Madách is forced to economize much more in the selection of historical scenes. The play's dialectical structure becomes therefore much clearer than the intended pattern in Hugo's work. By trying to be all-inclusive, to show various cultures in different stages of development, the French writer presents a more fragmented and diffuse picture.

At the end of Madách's drama Eve's pregnancy renders her husband's suicide futile and thus assumes a very different function from what Hugo relates in "Le Sacre de la femme," possibly his translation into lyrical poetry of his anger over the 1854 Papal Bull on the Immaculate Conception. The final reappearance of the Lord and Lucifer's admission of failure are organic consequences of the exposition of the Hungarian drama. In Hugo's work, however, the final poem with its vision of the day of judgment appears somewhat unmotivated after the celebration of man's technological and moral progress in "Plein Ciel" (In the Sky). The later inclusion of an introductory poem, "La Vision d'où est sorti ce livre" (The Vision Whence

This Book Came), establishes the function of "La Trompette du jugement," the conclusion of the first series, as an element of a greater
frame.

The optimism expressed in "Plein Ciel" and in the pivotal "Satyre"
poem marks the sharpest philosophical difference between the two
works. Hugo's vision of twentieth-century man soaring high above
the earth is a symbolic expression of his faith in the future and in the
role of science in the advancement of humanity. It is noteworthy that
Lamartine, trying to illustrate the "perfectible destiny" of the human
soul, likewise included a description of a flying machine in his epic.[28]
Such simple faith was impossible for the Magyar author after Világos
and in view of Hungary's centuries of struggle for national and cultural survival. The Phalanster scientist, optimistically building a
"brave new world," does not succeed: the last humans on earth vege-
tate in a frozen desert under a dying sun. And man's flight through
space, at first glance a strong parallel, is in fact radically different in
its implication. In Madách's play it is Lucifer's endeavor to pull
Adam away from the positive powers of nature. Life can be retained
only by returning to earth. This is the exact opposite of what has been
described as the central motif in Hugo's narratives: Adam must as-
cend rather than descend to face his ultimate contest.[29] The Lord's
final admonition to Adam demands an attitude that is a far cry from
the French belief in a better future.

The different titles chosen by the two authors are indicative of
their similarities and differences. For Madách, in his "tragedy of
man," each individual is another reincarnation of the same Adam,
and his eternal struggle is essentially tragic. Hugo, after considering
La Légende de l'humanité (The Legend of Mankind) and *La Légende
de l'Homme* (The Legend of Man), decided to place the emphasis on
history, not on individual man or mankind. But the singular of
légende stresses the attempt to view the multitude of centuries as aspects of the same general development, the "movement toward the
light."

Despite the universality Hugo aimed for, there are many references to French history and present conditions of the country.
Madách, on the other hand, carefully avoided the inclusion of anything specifically relating to his homeland, except for an incidental
allusion to Hunyadi. Yet Hungarians have always seen this work as
particularly expressive of their culture, and the encouragement to
strive and have faith in the face of a hopeless situation has inspired
generations. Hugo, reflecting a somewhat different outlook, was like-

wise to become a source of inspiration for his countrymen, even in France's darkest hours.

La Légende des siècles and *Az ember tragédiája*, written almost simultaneously in the relative isolation of Guernsey and Alsósztregova, are the clearest and most outstanding examples of the Romantic *poème d'humanité*.

III　*Madách and the Hungarian Romantic Tradition*

The experiences that contributed to the lessening of the German cultural influence in Hungary—although it is still quite obvious in Madách—also separated Magyar writers from the optimism of much of contemporary French literature. In this respect, *Az ember tragédiája* is truly Hungarian. While the play should not be considered merely a *drame à clef*, offering mainly cleverly disguised comments on Hungary's political and social conditions, Madách's view of world history is certainly colored by what he saw in his own country. And as a Hungarian, he shared in an experience not generally known to anyone belonging to a major nation: the concern for the survival of the nation and its culture, representing such a small and linguistically isolated entity. But Hungary and the Magyars had prevailed over the centuries, and thus the final words of the Lord are an expression of national sentiment as well as an appeal to all mankind.

So Madách's drama is both the realization of the possibilities of the European *poème d'humanité* with its universal message and a literary work that is representative of Hungarian culture. To be sure, he was the first and only major writer in Hungary to utilize this Romantic genre, but his way had been paved by others in the development of Magyar literature.

Miklós Zrínyi had focused on national history when he wrote his monumental epic *Szigeti veszedelem* (The Siege of Sziget) in 1645–46. But he, too, had presented human events in a metaphysical framework. By viewing the heroic defense of Szigetvár as part of a divine plan for mankind, he found a positive interpretation for a grim occurrence in the past. The Turkish troops, vastly outnumbering the Hungarian defenders, eventually emerged victorious, but Zrínyi elevated the defeated above the conquerors and—like Madách—conveyed a universal message as well.

Riedl suggests that Ferenc Kölcsey's pessimistic poem "Vanitatum vanitas" also prepared the ground for Madách's play.[30] The perspective that views the greatest battles as no more significant than a cockfight, self-sacrificing virtue as a dream, and the deaths of Socrates, Cato, or Zrínyi as acts of insanity is echoed in Lucifer's historic visions.

Mihály Vörösmarty used a symbolic drama as the medium for philosophical discussion. Even though the tone and spirit of his *Csongor és Tünde* is closer to Madách's *Tündérálom* fragment than to *Az ember tragédiája*, it may have had some impact on his choice of the dramatic mode as a vehicle for his views. And the words of the Philosopher whom Csongor asks for the right way to Fairyland and to his beloved Tünde could have been spoken to Adam: "Wake up, or, if it is better to dream on, go dream away your dream; for reality is a false hope." Csongor, quite in the spirit of Madách's hero, replies, "Destroy me not; this one wish gives me life." [31] But Csongor eventually has a happy reunion with Tünde; Adam's final encounter with Eve in the desolation of the ice region is the devastating culmination of his dreams.

Closer to the spirit of Madách's drama is Vörösmarty's poem "Gondolatok a könyvtárban" (Thoughts in the Library). The contrast between a book's paper and the rags from which is was made leads to reflections about history and man's destination:

> Loyalty, friendship tell their tale on a page
> Made from the clothes of base, treacherous perjurers.
> Hideous falsehood everywhere!
> The deathly picture of the pale leaf
> Condemns the written letters.
> Rags of countries! Your name is a library.
> But where is the book that leads to the goal?
> Where is the happiness of the majority?—Has the
> World advanced because of books? [32]

Yet we must strive, and the final message to Adam in Madách's play is very similar to Vörösmarty's admonition: "What is our task in life? To strive for the noblest goals with all our power." Man's responsibility is to advance humanity, and despite the gloomy experiences of the past, hope persists that there will be a future.

This hope is echoed in Petőfi's long poem "Az apostol" (The Apostle). Although the protagonist is destroyed by the brutality of the reigning powers and by the apathy or hostility of the masses, his life will not have been in vain. Mankind is progressing, and great men and great ideas contribute to the development of the human race, but

it is everybody's responsibility to do his share. Szilveszter, Petőfi's
hero, reflects on his role in life: a small grape needs a whole summer
and thousands of sunrays to ripen. The world requires much more.
The millions of rays that help to develop and ripen the world are the
souls of great men. This view of the slow development of mankind
and of the role of the individual in the process, and the ideal of freedom as the only means to attain happiness, are voiced in Madách's
poème d'humanité as well.

Some interesting parallels also exist between *Az ember tragédiája*
and Arany's poem "Gondolatok a békekongresszus felől" (Thoughts
about the Peace Conference), inspired by the Frankfort gathering of
1850.[33] Eternal peace is impossible; the strong have always oppressed
the weak and will continue to do so. But that oppression will also
perpetually foster rebellion. The study of world history is a sad subject: nations spring up like bubbles and disappear again. The Roman
Empire furnishes an example of physical degeneration and spiritual
overcultivation. The stagnant and foul-smelling waters of such a lazy
society spawn billions of new sins. Work and wealth are far apart.
The rich have hardened into stone, and the poor have become apa-
thetic. Cheating is common and has been perfected to an art. The
family spirit has disappeared: women are selling their virtue and hus-
bands their wives, and close relatives kill each other. But then "the
wild blood and virtue of a barbarian people will burst forth" and
sweep away the decayed society. The vision at the end of the Roman
scene in Madách's drama seems an echo of these thoughts. Even the
society of the London scene shares some features with Arany's description. The lesson to be learned from this "sad subject" is one that
Madách might have found acceptable: "The wise God is the one who
gives the orders;/ Man's task is to stay human / Both in peace and
war." Man is to be a "worthy image of God and a patriot for his country."

Kölcsey and Arany, but especially Vörösmarty and Petőfi represent
the spirit of Hungarian Romanticism. Madách, then, is not only a
"disciple of French Romanticism" but also the heir to the Hungarian
Romantic movement. This has sometimes been disputed. Paul van
Tieghem attempts to show the difference between Romanticism in
Hungary and elsewhere by emphasizing that the Magyar trend is essentially psychological, moral, and dramatic; it does not tend toward
those long meditations on the fate of mankind that gave birth to great
poems in other countries "unless one extends it all the way to
Madách's *Az ember tragédiája*." [34] Most modern critics, from Barta to

Vajda and Németh, do indeed extend Romanticism that far. Sőtér makes the point quite forcefully: "Romanticism did not only continue in the period after 1848 but it, so to say, renewed itself altogether. . . . Imre Madách . . . carried to its peak the romantic attitude and thinking of the movement which had begun in the 1820s." [35] A brief look at Hungarian Romanticism might thus show Madách's work in its proper national as well as European context.

While stressing how relativistic the concept of movements or currents is, Henry Remak stated: "Recent research is moving away from the idea that the succession of literary periods corresponds to a predestined, violent swing of the pendulum. . . . Instead, it has emphasized the gradual transition between periods, the overlapping and the simultaneousness of contrasting literary phenomena." [36] This reminder seems particularly appropriate with respect to Hungarian Romanticism where the dialectic view would yield less satisfactory results than in other countries whose Romanticism may have sprung from the rebellion against prevailing literary trends, such as French Classicism or German Enlightenment. Hungarian Romantic writing incorporated the heritage of Enlightenment and retained a certain rationalistic tendency throughout. Similarly, Realism in Hungary did not develop in opposition to Romantic attitudes, but Realistic features can be detected in many outstanding examples of Magyar Romanticism. As the result of certain geographic, political, and cultural conditions, Romanticism in Hungary—like other trends—developed and flourished somewhat later than elsewhere. Any attempt at periodization and categorization is a questionable undertaking, but the following overview may be helpful in establishing a general frame of reference.[37]

Hungarian Romanticism began around 1817 when Károly Kisfaludy settled in Pest to become the center of a group of young writers. His almanac *Aurora* served as the mouthpiece for Romantic poets of the 1820s and early 1830s. The period started with Kisfaludy's determined rejection of German Sentimentalism and reached its peak with the 1837 opening of the National Theater in Pest. That time also marks the high point in the work of József Bajza and Mihály Vörösmarty who, together with Kisfaludy and Ferenc Kölcsey, are the main representatives of this phase.

A revival of Romantic tendencies came in 1845–46 and was characterized by the emergence of Petőfi as a major poet. The earlier Romanticists had been decidedly nationalistic, but now the political involvement was direct. Petőfi and the "Young Hungary" movement paved the way for the events of 1848, and the impact of Hungarian Romanticism on Kossuth's rhetoric is evident. After 1849 Romanticism survived and experienced a revival in the works of Mór Jókai and Zsigmond Kemény. But a Realistic trend, an undercurrent for some time before, made itself felt more strongly. The experience of Világos and the Bach period also left its mark on the literary production of the time.

The "Magyarization" of European Romanticism is obvious from the very beginnings of the movement. Kisfaludy's role was largely that of naturalizing the new literary genres. The eminent literary historian of the period Ferenc Toldy (Franz Schedel) credits *Aurora* with having introduced to Hungarian readers the romance, the ballad, the short narrative, and the verse novel. Kisfaludy tried to give a specific national character to these Romantic genres. But it fell to Vörösmarty's poetic genius to fill the new forms with superior poetry and to shape them into truly Hungarian literature. Kisfaludy had first achieved national fame in 1819 with his play *A tatárok Magyarországban* (The Tartars in Hungary), and he set an example for others by continuing to select themes from Magyar history.

While foreign impulses had played an important role in launching the Romantic movement in Hungary, native authors soon turned against the "negative influences" of German Romanticism. Bajza and Kölcsey were among the leaders in this struggle for cultural autonomy. In his article on "Nemzeti hagyományok" (National Traditions) of 1826 Kölcsey discussed matters of principle in literary philosophy, attempted an analysis of the Hungarian national character, and established a program for the writers of his era. He emphasized Magyar folk poetry as the model and inspiration for original national poetry.

After a period of writing sentimental poetry, Kölcsey rejected the sentiment of the "yearning of love" and matured as a poet by expressing in verse his sorrow over the sad state of his country. His development as a lyrical writer had led him from the lofty ideal of Classicism to experimentation with the folksong form and to Romantic poetry that conjured up the great images of the past in order to contrast them with the misery of the present. As Sőtér says, he "approached romanticism as a result of his encounter with reality and the burning questions of the day—rejecting in this way the lyrico-sentimental manner." [38]

Vörösmarty also turned to his country's ancient history in his epic poem *Zalán futása* (Zalán's Flight) of 1825. He discarded the sentimentalism of his earlier poetry and discovered Classical meter, especially the hexameter, as an extremely suitable mode of expression for the Hungarian language. *Zalán* deals with the early settlement of Hungary by the Magyars. But the poet's obvious sympathy for the title hero, Arpád's ultimately defeated Bulgarian opponent, makes for a somewhat diffuse point of view. Vörösmarty's introduction of the sphere of the fairies into his account of historic events is significant. In the next few years he would repeatedly return to escapist "fairy world" poetry, culminating in his outstanding *Csongor és Tünde* of 1831. But after *Zalán* he no longer combined the world of history with the realm of the fairies. Unlike Kölcsey, Vörösmarty had to "extricate himself from the fairyland of romanticism, from the heroic and Ossianic moods of the Hungarian prehistoric age, to be able to express new themes provided by reality." [39]

In the character of Csongor, Vörösmarty created the first truly Romantic hero in Hungarian literature, restless, daring, and persevering, constantly expressing unexpected desires and an unquenchable thirst for happiness. He is striving for harmony, and his own personality holds the conditions and possibilities for that harmony. Vörösmarty based this portrait on the heroes of Hungarian folktales, and the protagonists of Petőfi's *János Vitéz* and of Jókai's novels seem to have been inspired by him. Tihamér Sámson, the hero of Vörösmarty's narrative poem *Két szomszédvár* (The Two Neighboring Castles), is a different but equally Romantic prototype. He represents disharmony and agitation and has been marked by fate; superhuman agony and passion fill his soul. In Csongor, the character on the ascending scale, the emphasis was on the heroic element. The declining hero, typified in Sámson, having defied the forces of fate and society, is essentially tragic.

The attempt to maintain a balance between fantasy and reality is characteristic of the Hungarian Romantic movement. József Bajza, theorizing in 1833 on the novel, illustrates this intertwining of Romanticism and Realism. His views could easily apply to Madách's drama, too: "The poet should not look for the image of man and the individual but in the individual for that of humanity; in the features of ages and peoples, human deeds and aspirations must be reflected so that their roots be based on reality." [40] The time for the heroic poem or heroic epic is over; Bajza welcomes the novel as the vehicle for revealing reality. Poetry has moved closer to life and philosophy; calling upon man in his daily circle, it can deal with his personal relations. The heroic poem in a broad sense reveals the future in a beautiful dream; the novel speaks of reality and—through the portrayal of psychologically true characters and the depiction of life—acquaints the reader with the human soul.

The interest in "man in his daily circle" tied in with the discovery of folk poetry as an important source of inspiration. Much of Petőfi's important lyrical poetry shows this influence. The language and some of the themes of Arany's verse give evidence of his interest in folk culture. His epic poem *Toldi* of 1846 narrates the adventures of a fourteenth-century hero of popular tradition. It proved that one could draw a convincing psychological portrait by utilizing folk vocabulary and stanzas that followed Hungarian patterns.

Bajza's theories seem to have materialized in the novels of Baron József Eötvös. The first of them, *A karthausi* (The Carthusian) of 1839–41, is a mixture of enlightened humanitarianism and Romantic effusion. But the satirical masterpiece *A falu jegyzője* (*The Village Notary*) gives a realistic description of life in rural Hungary. The theme of social oppression touched upon here is then emphasized in the historical novel *Magyarország 1514-ben* (Hungary in 1514) about György Dózsa's rebellion.

Eötvös's choice of topics underscores the message of his essay on Victor Hugo: he saw literature as a means of instructing his readers and thereby improving social conditions. Sőtér sums up Eötvös's attitude and relates it to the work of other Hungarian Romanticists: "Romanticism served as a medium to unite ideas with poetry and thereby add to the effectiveness of both. Poetry in the service of ideas—ideas expressed by means of poetry and propagated: this is the great innovation of romanticism. . . . In Kölcsey and Vörösmarty, thought and lyricism, ideas and emotions emerged in perfect union. The poetry of Eötvös proceeded on the same path, and passionate idea, or idealized passion produced the revolutionary poetry of Petőfi as well. . . . Romanticism achieves . . . the aim to appeal to the broader masses and become a mobilizing art." [41]

"Passionate idea or idealized passion" is an apt description of Petőfi's poetry after 1846. His last great narrative poem, outlining the path of life of his "apostle," is a fitting climax for his poetic development. Folk poetry and Romanticism had formed a fruitful synthesis in his work, and the alternating themes of love and revolution finally merge in the tale of the visionary idealist who becomes a political martyr. "Az apostol" is a product of Hungarian Romanticism, but its message far transcends the limitations of national culture.

Mór Jókai demonstrated after 1850 that Hungarian Romanticism did not die with Petőfi at Segesvár. Jókai's Romanticism was based on nostalgia. The struggles of recent Hungarian history preceding 1848 furnished the material for his novels. In his view progress and the developments in his country were synonymous. His heroes were ready to suffer any hardship in order to bring an end to oppression. In fighting for the nation, they were also working for the progress of humanity. In reality, however, the union of progress and nation no longer existed after 1849, and Jókai's works clearly mark the end of a period.

Madách's drama can rightly be seen as the last crowning achievement of Hungarian Romanticism, and the parallels in *Az ember tragédiája* and the works by Kölcsey, Vörösmarty, Petőfi, and Arany are hardly accidental. Madách's turning to history—albeit world history rather than the past of his own country—his use of a protagonist reminiscent of both Csongor and Tihamér Sámson, his attempt to find in the individual the image of humanity (as Bajza had demanded), and his successful union of ideas with poetry all have roots in the Romantic movement in Hungary. His philosophical drama is no more art for art's sake than were the novels of Eötvös. He also tried to instruct through literature, but after the events he had witnessed, he shared neither the optimism of French writers nor the nostalgic Romanticism of Jókai.

Madách did not think of himself as a Romantic poet. Yet the Romanticism satirized in the London scene is not that of Kölcsey, Vörösmarty, or Petőfi. When Adam complains about the misrepresentations of the puppet show which reviews the history of mankind in a burlesque fashion, Lucifer refers to himself as "the father . . . of the new trend they call Romanticism" in whose distortions he finds his delight, and he lists various forms of human degradation that are presently being celebrated (200–201). This is the Romanticism of the *Vigils of Bonaventura* and E. T. A. Hoffmann, the German Romanticism Goethe called "unhealthy."

In light of the Hungarian Romantic tradition, it is not surprising to find elements of Realism in Madách's play, too. But European literature and many Hungarian authors had turned toward Realism by the time he penned his drama, and his *poème d'humanité* represents the end of a literary trend rather than being in its mainstream. Thus, the emphasis on socioeconomic problems in the London scene, the critical look at scientific and socialist utopia in the Phalanstery, the brutal description of the dog-eat-dog world of the Eskimo scene, the incorporation of recent findings or speculations in the natural sciences into a dramatic poem also reflect the changing times.

Yet Adam is the idealized Romantic hero whose place is in the epics and dramas that had discussed mankind's fate ever since Goethe's *Faust*, not in the novel that was to become the favorite genre of Realism. Madách's eloquent attack on the novel—ironically a genre that he considered to be typical of Romanticism—in his inaugural speech before the Kisfaludy Society in 1862 indicates how much he personified a movement that had come to an end.[42] It should be remembered that he formulated his criticism a generation after Bajza's discussion of the possibilities of the novelistic genre. As Sőtér points out, Madách voiced his views when Balzac, Stendhal, and Dickens had already published their masterpieces, and his very choice of a dramatic poem as the vehicle for his ideas—like Arany's selection of a verse epic for his *Toldi*—shows him as falling out of step with the trend of the time.[43] Similarly, his complaint in *Tündérálom* about poetry having fled from a period marked by railroads and steam engines, telegraph, newspapers, and gas lights, confirms his position as that of a late Romanticist.

Az ember tragédiája constitutes the end of an important Hungarian development. As the last great *poème d'humanité* in European literature, it is the culmination of a Romantic genre that could not be used again with any degree of artistry or success. *Az ember tragédiája* is the brilliant sunset of literary Romanticism.

CHAPTER 7

A Century Later: A Concluding Note

MORE than a hundred years have passed since the Kisfaludy Society greeted the reading of the first four scenes of *Az ember tragédiája* with enthusiastic applause. Hungary and the rest of Europe have undergone dramatic changes. Yet the popularity of Madách's drama in his native country has persisted undiminished. It took twenty years for the play to reach its first stage production, but ever since 1883 there have been many successful performances in Budapest and other Hungarian cities, including the notable open-air presentations in the cathedral square of Szeged. Even *Mózes* and *Csák végnapjai*, after some unsuccessful attempts to stage them, eventually met with public enthusiasm in Dezső Keresztury's theatrical adaptations.

Since 1861 edition after edition of *Az ember tragédiája* has made Madách's drama accessible to Hungarian readers. For generations, their image of Adam, Eve, and Lucifer had been shaped by Mihály Zichy's famous illustrations, reflecting the taste and mood of the late nineteenth century.[1] The expressive semi-abstract pictures by Endre Bálint published more recently demonstrate the change in artistic preference and attitude that has occurred.[2] This change is also obvious if one surveys the stage productions from Ede Paulay's emphasis on costumes and décor for the first performance at the National Theater to Tibor Komlos's soberingly abstract presentation of 1964. But while the modern reader may even discover Madách as a pioneer of today's science fiction[3] and not just as a popularizer of history in the fashion of the nineteenth century, it appears that Adam's journey through time has lost little of its appeal. The Hungarian public has come to agree with Arany's assessment of the tragedy as an "excellent work, both in conception and in composition."

Scholarly interest in Madách has matched the general popularity of his work. From the first reactions of Arany, Erdélyi, Greguss, and Szász, from the extensive studies of Morvay, Alexander, and Voinovich to the examinations of the drama by Barta, Lukács, and Sőtér, and to contemporary research as evidenced in the recent collection of critical essays under Károly Horváth's editorship, Hungarian scholars have looked into sources and parallels, poetic development and textual authenticity, questions of structure, genre, and periodization. The problem of interpretation has been the most vexing, however, and today's experts still argue along the lines of the Erdélyi-Arany dispute and disagree on the point of historical accuracy and on the basic pessimism or optimism of the play.

Obviously, the bias or ideological slant of each period and each reviewer has affected the approaches to Madách's work. Catholic critics continue to object to the Constantinople scene, and Socialists still echo Erdélyi's reservations about the Phalanstery. The positivistic attitude of the nineteenth century, the emphasis on total originality, and the willingness to overlook contradictions and weaknesses in the drama while emphasizing its philosophical significance and eternal message have given way to a broader view which sees Madách's work as relating to the trends of the period and as reflecting both its author's individual experiences and limitations and the general conditions of nineteenth-century Hungary. György Lukács, in his controversial attempt of 1955 to demolish the "Madách legend," pointed to the way in which the drama had been ideologically misused.[4] In the wake of his spirited attack on the universality of Madách's message, critics have increasingly stressed the importance of the play as a document of cultural history. Yet neither the scholarly community nor the general public has been willing to accept the argument that Madách's unquestionable class bias has invalidated his expression of that paradoxical Tertullianist faith that has supported Hungarians over the centuries.

In light of Madách's careful avoidance of any references to Hungarian culture in his drama, it is surprising that it has remained comparatively unknown abroad. The play has been performed in Austria—at the prestigious Burgtheater—Czechoslovakia, Germany, and Poland; and radio versions have been broadcast in Austria, France, Germany, Switzerland, and the United States. But the English-speaking world has taken little notice of it even though a number of translations have been available since 1908. On the other hand, these very translations may have interfered with the drama's success. As Thomas Mark rightly asserts, they are "conceived in that peculiar pidgin English that Victorian orientalists reserved for 'Englishing' the Code of Hammurabi."[5] None of the versions published so far comes close to the accomplishment of Jenő Mohácsi in his German translation that reflects a truly bicultural genius and uses Goethe's language as a guide.[6] One day, perhaps, English-speaking audiences and scholars alike will understand why one of Europe's last great Romanticists is still his nation's pride.

Notes and References

Chapter One

1. But even under the feudal system, a higher proportion of the population had the franchise than in England prior to 1832 or in France at any time before 1848. For details, see Edsel Walter Stroup, *Hungary in Early 1848* (Buffalo, 1977), pp. 49–50.
2. As C. A. Macartney points out, every single deputy to the Diet of 1861 was in arrears with his taxes. See *The Habsburg Empire* (New York, 1969), p. 500.
3. See his undated letter, spring 1838 (ÖM 2, 901).
4. Quoted in Imre Madách, *Összes művei*, ed. Pál Gyulai, 2nd ed. (Budapest, 1894), 1, xxxii.
5. No formal political parties existed in Hungary before 1847.
6. *De la centralisation* (Paris, 1842) and *Livre des orateurs* (Paris, 1844). See the attempt to reconstruct the catalog of books in his library in József Szücsi, "Madách Imre könyvtára," *Magyar Könyvszemle*, NS 23 (1915), 5–28.
7. See his article "Iparvéd-egyesület" (Industrial Protection Association), ÖM 2, 628–31.
8. See in particular the deeply pessimistic poem he sent his friend on February 7, 1857 (ÖM 2, 989–90).
9. Quoted in Constantin von Wurzbach, *Biographisches Lexikon des Kaiserthums Österreich*, 16 (Vienna, 1867), 229.
10. See Géza Voinovich, *Madách Imre és Az ember tragédiája* (Budapest, 1914), p. 168.
11. Gábor Kiss, as quoted in Wurzbach, p. 228.
12. *Imre Madách: Die Tragödie des Menschen*, 2nd ed. (Würzburg, 1943), p. 5.
13. Imre Baranyi details the impact of this journal on young Madách in *A fiatal Madách gondolatvilága (Madách és az Athenaeum)* (Budapest, 1963).
14. Madách's library contained the 1823 volume.

Chapter Two

1. "A lírikus Madách," in his collection *Válogatott tanulmányok* (Budapest, 1966), pp. 624–34. Bóka's approach to Madách is similar to that of János Barta in *Az ismeretlen Madách* (Budapest, 1931). See also Aurél Kiss, "A

lírikus Madách," *Madách-tanulmányok*, ed. Károly Horváth (Budapest, 1978), pp. 255–64.

2. "Madách Imre," *Irodalomtörténeti Közlemények*, 62 (1958), 268–69.

3. "Madách Imre," in his collection *Romantika és realizmus* (Budapest, 1956), p. 260.

4. See Imre Madách, *Válogatott művei* (Budapest, 1958), and *Álom a történelemről: Madách Imre és Az ember tragédiája* (Budapest, 1965).

5. "Madách Imre," *Irodalomtörténeti Közlemények*, 62 (1958), p. 256.

6. For a detailed discussion of the early dramas and prose see Béla Kamarás's dissertation *Madách Imre ifjúkori drámái és novellái* (Pécs, 1941).

7. See Voinovich, p. 60; Sőtér, *Romantika és realizmus*, pp. 245–48.

8. For Madách's self-identification with Zordy, see his letter of February 9, 1844, to Szontágh (ÖM 2, 962–63).

9. "The Resurrection of a Play," *The New Hungarian Quarterly*, 7 (1966), 212.

10. *Romantika és realizmus*, pp. 252–57.

Chapter Three

1. For a brief summary of the major trends in Hungarian Madách criticism and an attempt to give a new interpretation, see Thomas R. Mark, " 'The Tragedy of Man': Salvation or Tragedy?" *Acta Literaria Academiae Scientiarum Hungaricae*, 15 (1973), 291–308.

2. "Madách Imre. Az ember tragédiája," published in *Magyarország* in 1862, reprinted in Erdélyi's *Pályák és pálmák* (Budapest, 1886), pp. 440–87. References are to this edition. Erdélyi's castigation of Madách's view on socialism was recently echoed by Marxist critics.

3. Erdélyi, p. 484.

4. "Greguss Ágost titkári jelentése a Kisfaludy-Társaság XII.-dik közülésében," *A Kisfaludy-Társaság Évlapjai*, 1 (1862), 13–31.

5. Quoted in Mark, pp. 291–92.

6. Ibid., p. 292.

7. Ibid., p. 296.

8. "Az ember tragédiája," *Budapesti Szemle*, 124 (1905), 57–115.

9. "Die Weltanschauung in Madáchs 'Tragödie des Menschen,' " *Stimmen aus Maria-Laach*, 80 (1911), 14–28. See esp. pp. 23–24.

10. See his introduction to Madách, *Válogatott művei*, especially pp. 35–40. Similar views can be found in his *Nemzet és haladás: Irodalmunk Világos után* (Budapest, 1963), pp. 672–80, and in *Álom a történelemről*, pp. 75–82.

Chapter Four

1. It is interesting that the critics attacking the drama as anti-Christian either overlooked or misinterpreted this important passage. Thomas Mark, in

rejecting the "salvationistic" interpretations, dismisses these lines as "ambiguous" (p. 294).

2. *Összes művei*, ed. Gyulai, 1, xxxi.

3. Quoted in Frigyes Riedl, *Madách* (Budapest, 1933), p. 48.

4. As late as 1892, the Austrian censor declared in connection with the production of the play in Vienna: "Furthermore, the intonation of the revolutionary song 'Marseillaise' . . . may be permitted only with the provision that the singing of this tune is meant merely to serve as a means of characterizing the historic moment of the scene but not to glorify the tendency of said revolutionary song. Therefore, the words assigned to Adam at the end of the eighth scene that would support the latter interpretation will have to be stricken" (Antal Németh, *Az ember tragédiája a színpadon*, Budapest, 1933, p. 62).

5. See Riedl, pp. 46–47.

6. For Madách's attitude toward women, see also his 1864 Academy address "A nőről, különösen aesthetikai szempontból" (On Women, Particularly from an Esthetic Viewpoint), ÖM 2, 583–603.

7. The two Prague scenes obviously deal with the same period; the flight in space is clearly outside the realm of history.

8. Georg Wilhelm Friedrich Hegel, *The Philosophy of History*, trans. J. Sibree (London, 1900), p. 16.

9. Ibid., p. 18.

10. Ibid., p. 54.

11. Ibid., p. 29 *et passim*.

12. Ibid., p. 32.

13. Ibid., pp. 103–104.

14. Ibid., p. 457.

15. See Hegel, p. 334.

16. Ibid., p. 31.

17. Ibid., p. 32.

18. See Hegel, p. 32. Andor Sas, in "Madách és Hegel," *Athenaeum*, NS 2 (1916), 206–20, cites this parallel to prove Hegel's influence (p. 213). But similar statements occur in Shakespeare and Goethe, and Madách did not need Hegel for this idea.

19. Hegel, pp. 338–39.

20. See Hegel, p. 427.

21. Hegel applied the German verb "aufheben" to the mechanics of both the antithesis and the synthesis because of its double meaning, "abolish" or "elevate."

22. See Voinovich, pp. 271–73 and 442–46.

23. See Riedl, pp. 48–49. See also Baranyi, *A fiatal Madách gondolatvilága*, pp. 45–46.

24. See Imre Madách, *Az ember tragédiája* (Budapest, 1956), p. 17.

25. See Horváth, "Madách Imre," *Irodalomtörténeti Közlemények*, 62 (1958), 469.

26. See *Romantika és realizmus,* especially p. 269.

27. See "Hegel és magyar közönsége," *Minerva,* 11 (1932), 3–21, especially p. 19.

28. "Zum Shakespeares-Tag," *Goethes Werke: Hamburger Ausgabe,* 4th ed., 12 (Hamburg, 1960), 226.

29. He owned the 1843 edition of *Das Wesen des Christentums.*

30. See *Das Wesen des Christentums,* ed. Werner Schuffenhauer (Berlin, 1956), p. 31.

31. Ibid., pp. 35–37.

32. Ibid., p. 44.

33. Ibid., p. 51.

34. This acquaintance is often assumed. Voinovich and Károly Kardeván's "Madách és Büchner," *Irodalomtörténet,* 3 (1914), 408–409, cite parallels but rely on thoroughly revised editions published after 1863. For a detailed discussion, see my 1961 Innsbruck dissertation "Madáchs 'Tragödie des Menschen' in der Begegnung mit der deutschen Geisteswelt," pp. 227–47.

35. The Hungarian term "erő" means both "force" and "strength." Incidentally, Büchner urges man to recognize the "firm and untearable" thread that ties him to nature. See *Kraft und Stoff,* ed. Wilhelm Bölsche (Leipzig, 1932), p. 189.

36. *Kraft und Stoff,* pp. 149–50.

37. Ibid., p. 33.

38. Ibid., pp. 179–80.

39. Ibid., pp. 12 and 16.

40. *Romantika és realizmus,* p. 270.

41. Ibid., p. 269.

42. See "Az ember tragédiája," *Katolikus Szemle,* 11 (1897), 531–44.

43. See Prohászka, " 'Az ember tragédiája' s a Pesszimizmus," *Katolikus Szemle,* 37 (1923), 193–201.

44. See "Die Weltanschauung in Madáchs 'Tragödie des Menschen,' " *Stimmen aus Maria-Laach,* 80 (1911), 24.

45. *Immanuel Kant's Critique of Pure Reason,* trans. Norman Kemp Smith (London, 1929), p. 653.

46. Ibid., p. 631.

47. Ibid., p. 632.

48. *Kant's Critique of Practical Reason and Other Works on the Theory of Ethics,* trans. Thomas Kingsmill Abbott (London, 1927), p. 260.

49. Hegel, *Sämtliche Werke,* ed. Georg Lasson, 8 (Leipzig, 1919–20), 425. The second edition, on which Sibree's translation is based, has a significant change here: ". . . is only to be found in the contest which Ormuzd carries on with Ahriman and in which he will at last conquer" (*Philosophy of History,* p. 179).

50. *The Complete Short Stories of Mark Twain,* ed. Charles Neider (New York, 1958), p. 661.

51. Ibid., p. 663.

52. Ibid., pp. 678–79.

Chapter Five

1. *Az ember tragédiája*, tr. Károly Erdélyi (Budapest, 1914), p. 15.
2. *Lenaus Werke*, ed. Max Koch, 2 (Berlin, 1890), 87.
3. "Ungarische Bühnenwerke in Deutschland," *Ungarische Jahrbücher*, 18 (1938), 47.
4. "Der ungarische Faustdichter Emerich Madách," *Illustrirte Zeitung*, 1864, p. 356; Rudolf Gottschall, "Eine ungarische Faustiade," *Blätter für die literarische Unterhaltung*, 1865, p. 540. But even more recent publications use titles like the following: Otto zur Nedden, *Imre Madách: "Die Tragödie des Menschen": Eine ungarische Faustdichtung* (Duisburg, 1957), or Günther Mahal, "Bemerkungen zum 'Ungarischen Faust': 'Die Tragödie des Menschen' von Imre Madách," *Ansichten zu Faust* (Stuttgart, 1973), pp. 131–68. J. W. Smeed goes even further; he quotes the title of the play in German and cites only from Dóczi's 1891 German translation, stating: "Quotations are given in the original language, except in the cases of A. Tolstoi and Imry [*sic*] Madách. Here, since one of the main points made is the link with Goethe's *Faust*, I have quoted from German translations rather than in English" (*Faust in Literature*, London, 1975, p. v).
5. Eugen Zabel, "Die Tragödie des Menschen von Madách," *Zur modernen Dramaturgie, 2: Studien und Kritiken über das ausländische Theater* (Oldenburg, 1899), pp. 212–16.
6. *Az ember tragédiája és a Faust* (Budapest, 1929).
7. *Geschichte der ungarischen Litteratur* (Leipzig, 1909), p. 219.
8. Gotthold Ephraim Lessing, *Sämtliche Schriften*, ed. Karl Lachmann, 3rd ed., 3 (Stuttgart, 1887), 386.
9. *Madách Imre Költészetének jellemzéséhez* (Kolozsvár, 1882), p. 33.
10. Lessing, p. 380.
11. As Andrew Török correctly pointed out in a private communication, Lucifer's attempt to destroy Adam in the space scene is logically inconsistent since this happens within the dream.
12. Lessing, p. 389.
13. *The Fortunes of Faust* (Cambridge, England, 1952), p. 123.
14. Lessing, 13 (1897), 24.
15. ÖM 2, 788.
16. *Letters from Goethe*, trans. M. V. Herzfeld and C. A. M. Sym (New York, 1957), pp. 413–14.
17. Johann Wolfgang von Goethe, *Faust: A Tragedy*. Walter Arndt, trans., and Cyrus Hamlin, ed. (New York, 1976), p.8.
18. Ibid., p. 33.
19. Ibid., p. 294.
20. See Voinovich, p. 518.
21. "Az ember tragédiájáról," *Szépirodalmi Figyelö*, 1862, quoted in Voinovich, p. 520.
22. Goethe, *Faust*, p. 26.

23. Ibid., p. 10.
24. Ibid., p. 48.
25. Ibid., p. 45.
26. Ibid., p. 64.
27. Ibid., p. 68.
28. Ibid., p. 73.
29. Ibid., p. 303.
30. *Conversations of Goethe with Eckermann and Soret*, trans. John Oxenford (London, 1874), p. 554.
31. Goethe, *Faust*, p. 42.
32. Ibid., p. 14.
33. Ibid., p. 8.
34. Ibid., p. 9.
35. Ibid., p. 40.
36. Ibid., p. 294.
37. Ibid.
38. Ibid., p. 27.
39. Ibid., p. 7.
40. Ibid., p. 8.
41. "Ay, and the very mightiest of the mightiest!/I've stood beside the Throne of God above,/And shared with Him the glory that surrounds Him!" (36).
42. This passage is given in J. C. W. Horne's translation (4th ed., Budapest, 1970, p. 24) which is clearer in this instance.
43. Goethe, *Faust*, p. 34.
44. Voinovich, p. 339.
45. *Conversations of Goethe*, p. 251.
46. Goethe, *Faust*, p. 110.
47. Eugène Bencze, "La 'Tragédie de l'homme': Est-elle le 'Faust' hongrois?" *Revue de littérature comparée*, 14 (1934), 142–54.
48. Ibid., p. 153.
49. Ibid., p. 149.

Chapter Six

1. "Dämmerstunde der Romantik—im Schatten des Positivismus," *Acta Litteraria*, 15 (1973), 81–121.
2. Victor Hugo, *La Légende des Siècles. La Fin de Satan. Dieu.* Jacques Truchet, ed. (Paris, 1950), p. 3.
3. *Die Menschheitsdichtungen der französischen Romantiker Vigny, Lamartine, Hugo* (Darmstadt, 1908), p. 148.
4. László Juhász, *Un disciple du romantisme français: Madách et La Tragédie de l'Homme* (Szeged, 1930), p. 32.

5. Wolfgang Margendorff, *Imre Madách: Die Tragödie des Menschen*, 2nd ed. (Würzburg, 1943), p. 1.

6. *Madách Imre* (Budapest, 1942), pp. 101–108.

7. Sőtér, *Romantika és realizmus*, especially pp. 258–59; Károly Horváth, "Az ember tragédiája mint emberiség-költemény," *Madách-tanulmányok*, pp. 27–46.

8. Enikő Molnár Basa, "The Tragedy of Man as an Example of the Poème d'Humanité" (Diss. University of North Carolina, 1972).

9. Ibid., p. 133.

10. Alfred de Vigny, *Oeuvres Complètes: Poésies* (Paris, n.d.), p. 193.

11. Alphonse de Lamartine, *Oeuvres: Poésies: La Chute d'un ange* (Paris, 1885), p. 2.

12. Alphonse de Lamartine, *Oeuvres: Poésies: Jocelyn* (Paris, n.d.), p. 5.

13. See Jean Bourilly, "Mickiewicz and France," *Adam Mickiewicz in World Literature: A Symposium*, ed. Wacław Lednicki (Berkeley, 1956), p. 258.

14. *World Drama from Aeschylos to Anouilh* (New York, n.d.), pp. 480–81.

15. Maria Csonka Farnek, "Imre Madách's 'The Tragedy of Man' and Wilhelm Jordan's 'Demiurgos': A Comparison" (Diss. State University of New York in Buffalo, 1970).

16. For details, see Otto Süpek, "L'Influence de Victor Hugo en Hongrie à l'époque des réformes," *Actes du IVe Congrès de l'Association Internationale de Littérature Comparée* (The Hague, 1966), 2, 1154–60.

17. Only this series—complete in itself—will be considered for the present comparison, not the supplements of 1877 and 1883 or the fragments *Dieu* and *La Fin de Satan*.

18. *Étude sur l'influence de la littérature française en Hongrie* (Paris, 1902), note on p. 349, quoted in Juhász, p. 10.

19. Voinovich, pp. 493–502.

20. See Juhász, especially pp. 32–38.

21. See György Mihály Vajda, "L'élément européen et hongrois dans la 'Tragédie de l'Homme,'" *Acta Litteraria*, 15 (1973), 337–46, and Mihály Szegedy-Marszák, "Life-Conception and Structure in 'The Tragedy of Man,'" in the same issue, pp. 327–35.

22. Jean Rousselot, in the preface to his Madách translation, refers to *La Fin de Satan* but does not mention *La Légende des siècles*. See *La Tragédie de l'Homme* (Budapest, 1966), pp. 5–30.

23. "Que le livre lui soit dédié;/Comme l'auteur lui est dévoué." (ÖM 2, 809).

24. Vajda, p. 343.

25. Naomi Schor, "Superposition of Models in *La Légende des Siècles*," *Romanic Review*, 65 (1974), 42–51.

26. Hugo, *La Légende des Siècles*, p. 4.

27. See Juhász, p. 44.

28. See *La Chute d'un ange*, "Huitième vision."

29. See Richard B. Grant, *The Perilous Quest: Image, Myth, and Prophesy in the Narratives of Victor Hugo* (Durham, N.C., 1968).

30. Riedl, p. 18.

31. Translated by D. Mervyn Jones in *Five Hungarian Writers* (Oxford, 1966), p. 125.

32. Ibid., p. 152.

33. See Riedl, pp. 21–23, for a discussion of this poem.

34. *Le Romantisme dans la littérature européenne* (Paris, 1948), p. 237.

35. *The Dilemma of Literary Science*, trans. Éva Róna (Budapest, 1973), p. 169.

36. "West European Romanticism: Definition and Scope," *Comparative Literature: Method and Perspective*, N. P. Stallknecht and H. Franz, ed., rev. ed. (Carbondale, Ill., 1973), p. 290.

37. This sketch relies heavily on Sőtér's discussion of "Hungarian Romanticism," *The Dilemma of Literary Science*, pp. 212–39.

38. Ibid., p. 219.

39. Ibid.

40. Ibid., pp. 227–28.

41. Ibid., p. 231.

42. "Az aesthetika és társadalom viszonyos befolyása," ÖM 2, 569–82. See especially pp. 576–78.

43. *Romantika és realizmus*, p. 237.

Chapter Seven

1. The Magyar Helikon edition, Magda Erdős, ed. (Budapest, 1958, second ed., 1960) still featured Zichy's illustrations.

2. See the Szépirodalmi Kiadó edition, József Szabó, ed. (Budapest, 1972).

3. See George Bisztray, "Man's Biological Future in Hungarian Utopian Literature," *Canadian-American Review of Hungarian Studies*, 3 (1976), 3–13, and György Radó, "Hungarian Science Fiction 1860," *SF Tájékoztató*, No. 6, 1972, pp. 41–44.

4. See György Lukács, "Madách tragédiája," *Szabad Nép*, 27 March and 2 April, 1955.

5. Thomas R. Mark, "Madách Revisited: Toward a New Translation of the *Tragedy of Man*," *Canadian-American Review*, 4 (1977), 145–54. Judging from the sample of Mark's translation provided here, its publication would fill a sorely felt need.

6. *Die Tragödie des Menschen* (Budapest, 1933, new ed., 1957).

Selected Bibliography

PRIMARY SOURCES

1. Collected Editions

Összes művei. Edited by Pál Gyulai. 3 vols. Budapest: Athenaeum, 1880. Second edition: 1894–95. Important as the first collected edition, but not quite complete and lacking critical apparatus.

Összes művei. Edited by Gábor Halász. 2 vols. Budapest: Révai, 1942. The most complete edition to date, containing literary works, articles and speeches, and correspondence. The critical apparatus is sketchy. Occasional mistakes and omissions make this edition not completely reliable.

Válogatott Munkái. Edited by Menyhért Palágyi. Budapest: Lampel Róbert, 1902. This selection contains some poetry and *Az ember tragédiája.* A complete list of the passages corrected by Arany is included.

Válogatott művei. Edited by István Sőtér. Budapest: Szépirodalmi Könyvkiadó, 1958. A reliable edition of selected works, containing some poetry, articles and speeches, dramatic fragments and dramas, a few letters, but no prose fiction. Helpful introduction and some explanatory notes.

Összes levelei. Edited by Géza Staud. 2 vols. Budapest: Madách Színház, 1942, The most complete edition of his correspondence in chronological order. The editor's comments are helpful. In contrast to Halász, Staud has modernized spelling and punctuation throughout.

2. Individual Editions

The number of separate editions of *Az ember tragédiája* is so great that a complete listing would not be useful. Therefore, only first editions and selected editions of special importance are listed below.

A civilizátor. Edited by Géza Voinovich. Budapest: Magyar Munkaközösség, 1938.

Az ember tragédiája. Published by Kisfaludy-Társaság. Pest: Gusztáv Emich, 1861. Second edition: 1863. Third edition: Pest: Athenaeum, 1869.

———. Edited by Bernát Alexander. Budapest: Athenaeum, 1900. Five revised editions until 1928. Extensive annotations, concluding essay, and bibliography made this a popular and useful edition. Alexander's comments reflect his era.

———. Edited by Vilmos Tolnai. Budapest: Magyar Irodalmi Társaság,

1923. Second revised and enlarged edition: 1924. The first critical edition.
————. Edited by József Waldapfel. Budapest: Szépirodalmi Könyvkiadó, 1954. A popular standard edition. An important introduction presents the Marxist position. Some explanatory notes and a list of the passages corrected by Arany.
————. Edited by Magda Erdős. Budapest: Magyar Helikon, 1958. The afterword by József Révai is of interest for its reinterpretation of the work in light of the 1956 events.
————. Facsimile edition. Budapest: Akadémiai Kiadó, 1973. Careful reproduction of the original manuscript.
Csák végnapjai. Edited and revised by Dezső Keresztury. Budapest: Magvető Könyvkiadó, 1969.
Csák végnapjai. Mózes. Edited and revised by Dezső Keresztury. Budapest: Magvető Könyvkiadó, 1972.
"A Csák végnapjainak első változata." Edited by Kálmán Bene. *Madáchtanulmányok.* Edited by Károly Horváth. Budapest: Akadémiai Kiadó, 1978, pp. 389–498. The original version of *Csák végnapjai.*
Lant-virágok. Pest: Füskúti Landerer Lajos (Printers), 1840.
Lant-virágok. Revised by Ödön Wildner and edited by Jenő Sugár. Budapest: Korvin, 1922.
Mária királynő. Revised by Miklós Gyárfás. Budapest: Szépirodalmi Kiadó, 1972.
Mózes. Edited and adapted for the stage by Dezső Keresztury. Budapest: Magvető Könyvkiadó, 1966.

3. English Translations
The Tragedy of Man. Translated by William N. Loew. New York: Arcadia Press, 1908.
————. Translated by Charles Henry Meltzer and Paul Vajda. Budapest: Vajna György, 1933. Subsequent Hungarian editions: Budapest: Corvina Press. Fourth and final edition, 1960. American edition: New York: Macmillan, 1935.
————. Translated by Charles Percy Sanger. London: Hogarth Press, 1933. Sydney, Australia: Pannonia Press, 1955.
————. Translated by J. C. W. Horne. Budapest:•Corvina Press, 1963. Fourth edition, 1970.
————. Translated by Joseph Grosz. Portland, Oregon: Irene Taylor (Printers), 1965.

SECONDARY SOURCES

1. Studies in English
Bisztray, George. "Man's Biological Future in Hungarian Utopian Literature." *Canadian-American Review of Hungarian Studies,* 3 (1976), 3–13.

Part of this brief article is devoted to the Phalanstery scene of *Az ember tragédiája*.

Gyárfás, Endre. "Imre Madách (1823–1864)." *Books from Hungary*, 6, No. 2 (1964), 4.

Hevesi, Alexander. "Madách and 'The Tragedy of Man.' " *The Slavonic and East European Review*, 9 (1930), 391–402. General introduction, later utilized for the preface to the American edition of the Meltzer-Vajda translation.

Hubay, Miklós. "Why is 'The Tragedy of Man' a Modern Play?" *Hungarian P.E.N.*, No. 6, 1965, pp. 29–35.

Keresztury, Dezső. "The Resurrection of a Play." *The New Hungarian Quarterly*, 7 (1966), 209–12. Brief discussion of *Mózes*.

Lesér, Esther H. "A Hungarian View of the World, Expressed in a Faustian Tragedy: Some Considerations upon Madách's *The Tragedy of Man*." *Canadian-American Review of Hungarian Studies*, 5, No. 2 (1978), 43–51. Madách's drama is discussed in its relationship to Goethe and Hegel.

Lotze, Dieter P. "From the 'Goethe of Széphalom' to the 'Hungarian Faust': A Half Century of Goethe Reception in Hungary." *Canadian-American Review of Hungarian Studies*, 6, No. 1 (1979), 3–19. A segment of this discussion of Goethe's impact on Hungarian Romanticism deals specifically with Madách's play.

———. "Madách's *Tragedy of Man* and the Tradition of the 'Poème d'Humanité' in European Literature." *Neohelicon*, 6, No. 1 (1978), 235–54. See Chapter 6 of this monograph.

———. "Madách's *Tragedy of Man*: Lessing Echoes in 19th Century Hungary?" *Lessing Yearbook*, 11 (1979), 133–41. A more detailed discussion of the thematic and philosophic parallels touched upon in Chapter 5 of this monograph.

———. "The 'Poèmes d'Humanité' of Guernsey and Alsó-Sztregova: Victor Hugo's *La Légende des Siècles* and Imre Madách's *The Tragedy of Man*." *Neohelicon*, 5, No. 2 (1977), 71–81. See Chapter 6 of this monograph.

Mark, Thomas R. "Madách Revisited: Toward a New Translation of the *Tragedy of Man*." *Canadian-American Review of Hungarian Studies*, 4 (1977), 145–54. A brief discussion of the play and of special problems of translation, and the text of the first scene in Mark's unpublished English version.

———. " 'The Tragedy of Man': Salvation or Tragedy?" *Acta Litteraria Academiae Scientiarum Hungaricae*, 15 (1973), 291–308. Stimulating discussion of the discrepancy between the concepts of tragedy and salvation in the drama. Review of critical opinions and attempt at new interpretation.

Radó, György. "Hungarian Science Fiction 1860." *SF Tájékoztató*, No. 6, 1972, pp. 41–44.

Reményi, Joseph. "Imre Madách." *National Theater Conference. Bulletin*, 12 (1950), 6–26. Reprinted in Reményi, Joseph. *Hungarian Writers and Literature*, August Molnár, ed. New Brunswick, N.J.: Rutgers University Press, 1964, pp. 127–45. A brief general introduction to Madách and his work and a synopsis of *Az ember tragédiája*.

Szegedy-Maszák, Mihály. "Life-Conception and Structure in 'The Tragedy of Man.'" *Acta Litteraria Academiae Scientiarum Hungaricae*, 15 (1973), 327–35. Madách's drama as seen in the framework of nineteenth-century European literature.

Sőtér, István. "Imre Madách's 'The Tragedy of Man.'" *The New Hungarian Quarterly*, 5 (1964), 56–66. Brief but insightful discussion of the play.

Wojatsek, Charles. "The Philosophical and Ethical Concept of the Tragedy of Man." *Études Slaves et Est-Européennes*, 6 (1961), 210–27. Interesting though traditional discussion.

In addition, two unpublished American doctoral dissertations deal with Madách:

Basa, Enikő Molnár. "*The Tragedy of Man* as an Example of the Poème d'Humanité: An examination of the Poem by Imre Madách with Reference to the Relevant Works of Shelley, Byron, Lamartine and Hugo." University of North Carolina, 1972.

Farnek, Maria Csonka. "Imre Madách's 'The Tragedy of Man' and Wilhelm Jordan's 'Demiurgos': A Comparison." State University of New York in Buffalo, 1970.

2. Studies in Hungarian

Only a few titles of special importance are listed below since the number of Hungarian publications on Madách is too vast to make a complete listing feasible or helpful. (A Madách bibliography for the years 1964–1972 only, as prepared by the Balassi Bálint Library of Nógrád County, has 212 separate entries.) Bibliographical information may be found in several of the Madách editions listed above and in most of the studies below, especially in Voinovich (very complete listing of older titles), Barta, Sőtér, and Kántor (the most significant Hungarian studies from 1862 to 1965).

Balogh, Károly. *Madách, az ember és a költő*. Budapest: Vajna György, 1934. Biography and an attempt to arrive at an integrated interpretation of Madách's work.

Barta, János. *Madách Imre*. Budapest: Franklin-Társulat, 1942. Biography and scholarly discussion of Madách's work. Important determination of the playwright's position as a late Romanticist in the context of European literature.

Horváth, Károly. "Madách Imre." *Irodalomtörténeti Közlemények*, 62 (1958), 247–78; 462–502. Important study of Madách's work and the impact of his times on it.

————, ed. *Madách-tanulmányok*. Budapest: Akadémiai Kiadó, 1978. Important collection of articles on *Az ember tragédiája,* Madách's position in European and Hungarian literature, stage productions, his poetry and other works, his political views, and family history. Also contains the 1843 version of *Csák végnapjai.*

Kántor, Lajos. *Százéves harc "Az ember tragédiájá"-ért.* Budapest: Akadémiai Kiadó, 1966. An overview of critical positions from Arany to the present.

Lukács, György. "Madách tragédiája." *Magyar irodalom—magyar kultúra.* Budapest: Gondolat Kiadó, 1970, pp. 560–73. The controversial 1955 attempt to destroy the "Madách legend." The contradictions in Madách's work are seen as reflecting class bias. *Az ember tragédiája* is valuable as a historic document, not as a work of art.

Morvay, Győző. *Magyarázó tanulmány "Az ember tragédiájá"-hoz.* Nagybánya: Molnár Mihály, 1897. Significant as the first detailed study of Madách's drama.

Németh, Antal. *"Az ember tragédiája" a színpadon.* Budapest: Székesfőváros, 1933. An account of fifty years of stage presentations of Madách's play in Hungary and abroad.

Németh, G. Béla. "Madách Imre." *Türelmetlen és késlekedő félszázad: A romantika után.* Budapest: Szépirodalmi Kiadó, 1971, pp. 150–63. Important attempt to determine Madách's position with respect to the cultural trends of his century.

Radó, György. "Az ember tragédiája a világ nyelvein. 1–6." *Filológiai Közlöny,* 10 (1964), 313–53; 11 (1965), 93–124; 12 (1966), 67–108; 14 (1968), 75–111; 17 (1971), 382–403; 18 (1972), 47–71. Extensive survey of the translations of Madách's drama.

Riedl, Frigyes. *Madách.* Budapest: Királyi Magyar Egyetemi Nyomda, 1933. This slim but excellent study was compiled by Riedl's students from his lectures on Madách.

Sőtér, István. *Álom a történelemről: Madách Imre és Az ember tragédiája.* Budapest: Akadémiai Kiadó, 1965. Important study of *Az ember tragédiája* by one of the greatest authorities on Madách. Attention to the role of the play in the poet's artistic development and to its ties to the period.

———. "Madách Imre." *Romantika és realizmus.* Budapest: Szépirodalmi Könyvkiadó, 1956, pp. 217–93. Significant attempt to relate Madách's work to Hungarian and European literary trends and to developments in Hungary.

Voinovich, Géza. *Imre Madách és Az ember tragédiája.* Budapest: Franklin-Társulat, 1914. Second edition, 1922. Though outdated in some ways and occasionally repetitious, this is a classic study that offers a wealth of information.

Waldapfel, József. "Madách igazáért." *Irodalmi tanulmányok.* Budapest: Szépirodalmi Könyvkiadó, 1957, pp. 440–66. A Marxist approach to *Az ember tragédiája,* emphasizing the literary rather than philosophical importance of the work.

Index

A *falu jegyzője* (Eötvös), 149
A *karthausi* (Eötvös), 149
"A magyar nemes" (Petőfi), 37
A *tatárok Magyarországban* (Kisfaludy), 147
Academy of Sciences, 18, 24, 27, 28, 30, 31, 44
Ahasvérus (Quinet), 133
Alsósztregova, 21, 22, 26, 28, 138, 143
Ampère, Jean-Jacques, 125
Andersen, Hans Christian, 130
Andrássy, Gyula, 22
Andrássy, Manó, 22
Angelo (Hugo), 137
"April Laws" of 1848, 18, 20, 45
Arabian Nights, 30
Arany, János, 15, 27, 29, 31, 36, 41, 44, 46, 47, 55, 96, 145, 149, 150, 151, 152
Aristophanes, 26, 43
Arndt, Walter, 159n17
Athenaeum, 31
Augustine, Saint, 77, 89, 101
Austria, 16, 17-18, 19-20, 25, 35, 41, 45, 87, 153, 157n4; *See also* Bach Regime, Compromise, *Gesamtmonarchie*, Habsburg, Vienna, War of 1848-49
Aurora, 31, 146, 147
"Az apostol" (Petőfi), 144-45

Bach Regime (Bach, Alexander), 20, 26, 43, 87, 137, 147
Bajza, József, 15, 29, 31, 33, 147, 148, 149, 150, 151
Balassagyarmat, 23, 26, 42, 73; *See also* Nógrád County
Bálint, Endre, 152
Balzac, Honoré de, 151
Bánk bán (Katona), 28
Baranyi, Imre, 155n13, 157n23
Barta, János, 131, 132, 138, 145, 152, 155n1
Basa, Enikő Molnár, 131, 138
Batthyány, Lajos, 18, 19

Bencze, Jenő, 127-28
Benedek, Marcell, 72-73
Bérczy, Károly, 22, 28
Bismarck, Otto von, 136
Bisztray, George, 162n3
Bóka, László, 34
Bourilly, Jean, 161n13
Braha, Tycho, 61
Brecht, Bertolt, 44
Breitschwert, Johann Ludwig Christian, 75
Büchner, Ludwig, *91-96*, 130
Buda, 18
Budapest, 135, 152
Burke, Edmund, 75
Butler, Eliza Marian, 109
Byron, George Noël Gordon, 29, 101, 106, 110, 122, 130, 131-32, 134, 136, 137

Cain (Byron), 132, 137
Calderón de la Barca, Pedro, 89, 109
Candide (Voltaire), 30
Catholicism, 21, 38, 79, 83, 96-97, 100, 101, 104, 136, 140, 153
Centralist movement, 15, 16, 19, 23
City of God (Saint Augustine), 77
Classicism, 30, 127, 146, 147
Communist Manifesto (Marx), 86
Compromise with Austria, 15, 20, 22, 35, 41
Copernicus, Nicolaus, 83
Cormenin-Timon, Louis Marie de la Haye, 23
Cosmos (Humboldt), 30, 91
Critique of Practical Reason (Kant), 98
Critique of Pure Reason (Kant), 97-98
Cromwell (Hugo), 138
Csák, Máté, 41
Csák Maté (Kisfaludy), 41
Csongor és Tünde (Vörösmarty), 28, 46, 144, 148, 150
Cyprian, Saint, 109
Czesztve, 24, 25, 26

Soumet, Alexandre, 130, 131, 133
Spengler, Oswald, 118
Stendhal (= Henri Beyle), 151
Stephen, Saint. *See* István I
Storm and Stress, 105, 106, 129
Strindberg, August, 74
Stroup, Edsel Walter, 155n1
Süpek, Otto, 161n16
Szász, Károly, 72, 96, 112, 137, 138, 140, 152
Széchenyi, István, 18, 23, 30, 31, 45
Szeged, 152
Szegedy-Maszák, Mihály, 138
Székesfehérvár, 97
Szigeti veszedelem (Zrínyi), 143
Szigligeti, Ede, 29
Szontágh, Pál, 23, 24, 26, 27, 35, 60, 126
Sztregova. *See* Alsósztregova
Szücsi, József (= József Bajza), 155n6

Tertullian, 110, 153
Theodicy (Leibniz), 78
Thomas à Kempis, 29
Thököly, Imre, 21, 38
Toldi (Arany), 149, 151
Toldy, Ferenc (= Franz Schedel), 147
Tolstoi, Alexei, 159n4
Tompa, Mihály, 27
Török, Andrew, 159n11
Trachinian Women, The (Sophocles), 24, 42
Transylvania, 18, 19, 20, 25
Tudományos Gyüjtemény, 31
"Tündérálom" (Petőfi), 31
Turkey, Turks, 17, 19, 33, 143
Twain, Mark (= Samuel Langhorne Clemens), 102-103

Vác, 21
Vachot, Imre, 30
Vajda, György M., 138, 146

Valéry, Paul, 105
Van Tieghem, Paul, 145
Verbőczy. *See* Werbőczy
Verseghy, Ferenc, 15
Vienna, 18, 20, 107, 135, 157n4; *See also* Austria, Habsburg
Vigils of Bonaventura, The (Wetzel?), 150
Vigny, Alfred de, 123, 130, 131, 133
Világos, 19, 25, 142, 147
Voinovich, Géza, 41, 74, 87, 112, 125, 138, 152, 158n34
Voltaire, François Marie Arouet de, 29, 30, 109
Vörösmarty, Mihály, 15, 28, 30, 31, 33, 34, 46, 144, 145, 146, 147-48, 149, 150

Wagner, Richard, 135
Waldapfel, József, 87
Wallis, A.S.C. (= Adele Opzoomer), 105
War of 1848-49, 15-16, 19, 24-25, 34, 35, 41, 87, 147
Weber, Carl Julius, 130
Weltenmorgen (Hlatky), 136
Weltschmerz, 33, 65, 122
Werbőczy, István, 18, 31
Wilbrandt, Adolf von, 135-36

Young, Edward, 30
"Young Hungary" (*Fiatal Magyarország*), 16, 18, 146

Zabel, Eugen, 159n4
Zalán futása (Vörösmarty), 147-48
Zapolyai, János, 17
Zichy, Mihály, 152
Zilahy, Károly, 60
Zrínyi, Miklós, 143
Zsigmond (of Luxemburg), 33, 40
Zur Nedden, Otto, 159n4